UNDERSTA
AGING PAI

D0822317

This Book Presented

by

Nathan & Aaron Walker

CHRISTIAN CARE BOOKS

Wayne E. Oates, Editor

UNDERSTANDING AGING PARENTS

by
Andrew D. Lester
and
Judith L. Lester

THE WESTMINSTER PRESS
Philadelphia

Copyright © 1980 The Westminster Press

Book Design by Dorothy Alden Smith

First edition

Published by The Westminster Press®
Philadelphia, Pennsylvania

PRINTED IN THE UNITED STATES OF AMERICA
9 8 7 6 5 4 3 2 1

Library of Congress Cataloging in Publication Data

Lester, Andrew D
    Understanding aging parents.

    (Christian care books ; 8)
    Bibliography: p.
    1. Parents, Aged—United States.   2. Aged—Health
and hygiene.   3. Middle age—United States—Family
relationships.   I. Lester, Judith L., 1940–   joint
author.   II. Title.   III. Series.
HQ1064.U5L473   306.8'7   80–17832
ISBN 0–664–24329–0

Contents

Foreword

It has been customary to think of life in its developmental perspectives. The developmental tasks of children, adolescents, and young adults have been studied. But middle age has only recently been a subject for social research. One of the basic developmental tasks of middle age is learning how to relate creatively to our aging parents.

We, the authors, did not become aware that we had entered this period in life until (1) Judy's father retired early and, with her mother, moved to a retirement village in south Florida, and (2) Andy's father, now seventy-six, had two serious heart attacks and extensive surgery. Both sets of parents are involved in teaching us about the aging process and what it is like for middle-aged children to relate to aging parents. We have dedicated this book to them with the hope that it not only reveals what we have learned to this point, but will enlighten the path we follow in the future.

Since accepting the challenge to write this book, we have spent many hours studying the professional literature on aging (gerontology and geriatrics) in psychiatry, sociology, psychology, and medicine. We have learned much from this literary research. Just as important, however, are the friends and acquaintances who gave of their time and energy to teach us about their specific experiences with the process of aging and with elderly parents. They wrote thoughtful letters and essays, allowed us to tape lengthy interviews, raised questions about our rough drafts, and shared their observations. We have also learned from leading family life conferences and workshops where both middle-aged children and aging parents revealed thoughts and feelings about their relationship during this period of life. Other input came from persons we counseled who were struggling with problems related to elderly parents. For all these fellow pilgrims we are grateful!

Wayne Oates, editor of the Westminster Christian Care Books, has been our special friend and colleague for many years. We express our sincere appreciation for his usual faithfulness during the process of writing this book. His gentle, nudging support has been consistent and undergirding.

These pages include many illustrations. Each is an actual situation taken from the sources mentioned above. All data is accurate except the names, which have been changed to prevent identification.

Our prayerful hope is that you might find in these pages ideas that shed light on the uniqueness of the relationship you have with your aging parents. Our Christian faith calls us to honor our fathers and mothers. To understand them is to facilitate the growth necessary to attain this goal.

A.D.L. and J.L.L.

Louisville, Kentucky

1. Relating to Our Aging Parents

Life is filled with significant relationships. The primary ones are studied and written about extensively: mother/child, husband/wife, and parent/teenager, for example. However, the relationship between aging parents and middle-aged children has been largely ignored. Only infrequently has it been studied and described in either popular or professional literature. We feel that it deserves specific attention.

Human relationships change whether we like it or not. Our relationship to our parents, which remains crucial throughout our lives, is no exception. During infancy, childhood, adolescence, and young adulthood it takes different forms. Now we are middle-aged individuals and this relationship with our parents takes on additional features as they reach senior citizen status.

ACCEPTING OUR PARENTS' LIFE-STYLE

When we were teenagers and explored new life-styles, many of our parents had negative reactions. Did your choice of clothes, hairstyles, and friends cause conflict? Remember their anger and embarrassment about some of your behavior, your language, your choice of heroes, and even your political beliefs?

Now you may be in the same situation, but reversed. As parents grow older, they may become less concerned with the social pressures that dictated their lives during the middle years. They may begin to live in ways that are disturbing and upsetting to you. They may get involved in offbeat religion, join radical political causes, dye their hair, or spend money on seemingly foolish activities. Any of these choices may lead you to feel angry, embarrassed, or worried about what other people will say about *your* parents!

Once our parents thought we were *too young* to do, see, touch, taste, and feel certain things. Now we may think they are *too old* for the same things or to have the same freedom. Remember our fierce defense of our right to make our own decisions in those teen years? Remember how angry and resistive we felt toward those who thought they knew more than us? Maybe we can understand their feelings and grant them the right to adopt their own life-style and make their own choices at this point in their lives.

It is a temptation to be judgmental of our parents' choices, interfere with their plans, and control their lives. But what good can come of it? Why not celebrate their independence? Why not give loving support to their interests, listen to their philosophies, and enjoy their new experiences? If life is rich and enjoyable for our aging parents we, too, are blessed.

Our Emotional Response

Relating to our parents through this period of life will generate strong feelings that are not easy to understand, much less, communicate. These experiences will be described throughout the following chapters, but here is an overview.

Guilt

Guilt is a common experience for adults in mid-life as they deal with aging parents. Many circumstances create these guilty feelings. Geographic distance is one example. Not being present to help our aging parents creates guilt in us.

When her mother died, Beth lived in Pennsylvania, fifteen hundred miles away. She felt guilty over not being closer to home for two reasons. "Living away from home placed an added burden of guilt on me because I was not able to be with my father immediately after her death. Even worse, I had to leave to get back. My need to talk and express my thoughts and feelings with my dad was not met. He wasn't finished talking either."

Being geographically separated also creates guilt with reference to siblings who are at home shouldering the responsibility.

Sharon always felt a little guilt for living so far from her parents, but it multiplied immensely after her father died. Her sister bore the brunt of the mother's lengthy grief and depression. Guilt is compounded by the fact that Sharon's sister has openly committed herself and her family to "staying at home to take care of mother," with the implication that this is what *good* children do. Sharon's mother keeps suggesting to her, "If you really loved me, you would live closer and care for me."

You may feel guilty because not being near your parents resulted in some needs going unnoticed and unmet. Perhaps your guilt stems from decisions you could have influenced if you had been present.

Grief

Watching our parents age is to experience some anticipatory grief over their approaching death. When they enter a hospital or nursing home, our grief increases. Adult children may find it quite difficult to visit aging parents because their parents' losses sadden them. The coming separation provokes anxiety.

> At age ninety-two Richard's mother was now in a nursing home. She was experiencing not only physical deterioration but failure of her mental processes. Her conversation rambled. She was confused about who had been to see her. She accused Richard of not coming to see her although he went every day. Richard was an only child and his closeness to his mother made his grief over the loss of this relationship almost unbearable. He finally had to stop seeing her except once a week in order to keep his grief under control.

It is quite threatening to lose such a primary relationship. We will discuss this further in Chapter 7.

Gratitude and Affection

For those of us who are blessed with special parents whom we love dearly, their aging will spark within us strong feelings of affection and gratitude. To realize that they give so much, to appreciate the model their lives provide, to stand amazed at the love and acceptance offered us at every turn, is to give thanks! It is hoped that we will express our gratitude not only to God but to our parents. It will be meaningful to them to know of our appreciation for the gifts of life and love they bestowed upon us.

Wrestling with the Past

Personal history affects our present pilgrimage. This is particularly true as we relate to our parents during the aging process. Memories you have about growing up, even the young adult years, will give shape to your present feelings and actions.

If you felt that your parents gave themselves unselfishly to their parenting responsibilities and had your best interests at heart, you will respond positively. If you felt wanted, loved, accepted, and liked by your mother and/or father, you are more likely to forgive their mistakes and understand their weaknesses. You can respect them and consider it a privilege to care for them if they bestowed their blessings on you as a youth. It will be easy for you to "honor your father and your mother" (Ex. 20:12).

Some of you, however, did not experience love and acceptance from your parents. They withheld blessings, always demanded more, and rarely communicated that you were worth anything to anybody! Perhaps they even abused you physically or emotionally. Maybe their life-style is one you do not respect. How can you suddenly become a sweet, understanding son or daughter, ready to step in and help them through the aging process? Not very easily! Your negative feelings will interfere. If your parents have "provoked you to anger" (Eph. 6:4), it is difficult to honor them.

Many readers will identify with both positive and negative memories. Most parents are neither saints nor demons, but did the best they could, given their own problems, personalities, and backgrounds. This may leave you with ambivalent feelings about the past which confuse the present relationship. One visit is warm and positive, but the next may be distant and conflictual.

Frustrating as it may be, the past is difficult to change.

Human personality can and does change, but many middle-aged children experience frustration because their parent's personality is the same—yesterday, today, and seemingly forever!

Angela's father finds it difficult to express emotion and carefully controls his warm feelings. He learned early to cope with life aggressively. His gruffness hides his tenderness, and he could not express his love for Angela as she grew up. Now she would like to hear it, to somehow feel that he cares for her, but he is unable to make much change.

Some parents do mellow with age. Others just seem to harden and their negative characteristics become more pronounced. When change does occur it can be a blessing for both parent and child.

A forty-nine-year-old friend wrote us about such a change. "Mother had never been a very demonstrative person as far as affection, touching, or verbalizing love are concerned. However hard I tried in my adult years to get her to change she resisted, saying, 'When you haven't been brought up that way, it's hard.' When she became confined to a nursing facility, she began to show some of the loving tendencies I had hoped for all along. Finally she began to initiate 'love talk' and touching. I am grateful for that experience."

Changing Roles

Coming to grips with our past relationship to our parents becomes crucial as we deal with changing roles precipitated by the aging process. They parented us, now they need parenting—a strange reversal which can be uncomfortable. We asked our parents for advice, but now they consult with us.

They took us to choir practice, basketball games, and scouts. Now they need us to take them shopping and to the doctor. Once upon a time they gave us an allowance, now we may supplement their income.

Despite these changes in function we are still their children and they are still our parents. This means parent-child interactions may continue as if they were still thirty-five and responsible for us as teenagers. For example, your parents may have done without things so you could have what you needed. Now, even though it is unnecessary, they may still be sacrificing in order to make sure you keep what you have.

Mark's mother has "a very substantial savings account for the sole purpose of paying for a nursing home if needed." She lives at a much lower standard of living than is necessary, "bemoaning the cost of living and doing without many things she could afford." Both Mark and his sister can take care of her during the aging process and urge her to use some of the savings, but she resists. Why? "She constantly reminds us that she does not want us to have to use our money to take care of her. It is very frustrating!"

Our parents have always been involved in our lives, sharing our failures and being proud of our accomplishments. They still hurt when we have problems and get vicarious satisfaction from our successes. To let them continue sharing our lives can be a gift.

Benny is a successful professional. It used to embarrass him when his parents told others about his professional competence. He now recognizes the increased meaning which they experience when bragging about him. After all, they want folks to know that their life had been worthwhile. Instead of hiding his accomplishments, he now sends them copies of books and articles he has written. He also sends stories from local newspapers about his work.

As roles and functions change, it reminds our parents that they are losing autonomy and control of their own lives. For us to accept the change in roles, without demanding that these dynamics be reversed, is a way of continuing to respect and honor our parents. How you, as an adult in mid-life, will handle role changes will depend partly on how you handle the dependency issue.

The Dependency Issue

As parents age, and their increasing need for assistance becomes obvious, middle-aged children are called to deal with the dependency issue. What do we mean? Our mother and father joined God in creating us. For many years we were completely dependent on them. They fed, clothed, changed, bathed, nursed, and protected us. As we grew up we reached for independence. Ideally we found autonomy, established an identity apart from our parents, and then moved into an interdependent relationship with them. The question, then, concerns whether you made it or got stuck. Are you dependent, independent, or interdependent?

Some persons found it difficult to cut the apron strings. The natural development toward independence was blunted or short-circuited by (1) parents who were domineering, over-protective, or abusive; (2) traumatic events, such as prolonged illness; or (3) an underdeveloped sense of worth and esteem because of repeated failures or rejections in the community. In middle age these children may remain dependent financially, socially, geographically, or vocationally, but basically we are talking about emotional dependency.

The dependent adult child still does what he or she

knows the parents would like done. He thinks the way they want him to think. She believes and perceives the way her parents influence her. Dependent children still have a "one flesh" relationship with one or both parents. Obtaining acceptance and approval from parents is still a paramount concern.

Edwin will again be taking his family home this Christmas, not because anyone in the family wants to go, but because his mother demands it. "I know you will come because you have always loved me," she says. Edwin, forty-two, is afraid that if he does not go, his mother will interpret that he has stopped loving her. His dependence on her approval leaves him trapped by her every wish.

Pleasing parents, for the dependent child, is done as a "have to" rather than the "want to" of the interdependent child.

If you are still dependent on your parents, their aging will create additional problems. It will be difficult for you to allow them to lean on you because you are dependent on their strength. Realizing that they will die threatens your source of strength, nurture, and identity. You may find yourself panicked or immobilized by their growing dependency and their obvious mortality.

Now is your opportunity to break out of your dependency. To do so will allow you to relate creatively and supportively to your parents at a time when dependency needs to be reversed. A professionally trained minister or mental health worker can help you.

Perhaps you are one of those who fought hard for freedom and established a separate life. Independence is good, but some had to fight so hard they cannot move on to interdependence. They, too, are afraid, not of being abandoned, but of being swallowed up, used, or trapped. So they fight to remain separate. When parents need them it creates anxiety.

Getting "close" still feels dangerous. They may wish to help but cannot risk being vulnerable.

Actually these people are pseudoautonomous. In reality they have not attained the level of internal emotional freedom from their parents to establish a secure personal identity. That is why the dependency issue is revived when their parents age. To respond creatively to your parents through this period of their lives means risking interdependence.

2. Changes in Our Parents' Bodies

Physical changes are often the first reminders that our parents are aging. We may be jarred into this realization by a serious health problem, such as a stroke, heart attack, or broken hip. Others of us simply begin to notice that our parents' skin is more wrinkled, they walk more cautiously, and they do not hear as well. We begin to recognize how much impact physical changes and the fear of future physical problems are having on their lives.

Old age is not a disease! Nor does old age itself cause diseases that are common among older people. However, each system in the body is affected by the aging process. How fast it occurs and when it becomes noticeable vary from person to person. This aging process is affected by both genetic and environmental factors. The attitudes of the older person and those surrounding him or her may have a profound impact on the rate of the aging process.

Major Body Systems

Noticeable signs of aging include changes in appearance, functioning at a slower pace, less resistance to disease, vulnerability to accidents, slower recovery from illness, and less endurance. These signals occur because of changes in the major body systems.

Skin

The easiest way to identify older persons is by their skin. It becomes rough, wrinkled, and dry as a result of the breakdown of collagen. Dark pigmented lesions often appear. The skin is more easily bruised and more prone to develop cancers. Our culture's emphasis on youth and beauty makes this early sign of aging a badge that many older persons wear with shame.

Middle-aged adults can help aging parents by openly discussing the fact that changes in outward appearance do not make a person dysfunctional, unattractive, or unlovable. The middle-aged adult must also be aware that persistent skin problems may be a danger signal and need proper medical attention.

When Mark's mother came to visit recently, he noticed a growth on the side of her nose. When he asked about it, she indicated she was not worried "because a mole had always been there." At his insistence she had a biopsy. The growth turned out to be cancerous and she was able to get appropriate treatment. Afterward she admitted that her fear of cancer had led her to deny what was happening on her nose.

Bones

As bones become more porous they become more brittle, a fact that heightens the chance of fractures. These fractures heal more slowly in the elderly and often result in a limp, changed posture, or shortened stature. Walking more slowly, or with a shuffle, may be due to the stiffening of the joints.

Arthritis occurs when the joints become inflamed or the joint lining deteriorates.

Our parents feel more vulnerable to fractures and may express fears about tripping or falling. They have seen friends for whom a broken hip has begun a more rapid physical deterioration.

> Mrs. Read is eighty years old now, talking with us about breaking her hip when she was seventy-eight. "That hip breaking was the worst thing that has ever happened to me. . . . When I broke my hip it seems like I stepped over the line into another world. I never had anything that took as much out of me as that did!"

Poor eyesight contributes to this fear of falling and may cause changes in posture and gait. Older persons may be stooped and shuffling only because they are watching for dangerous terrain.

> Mrs. Read speaks again. "The broken hip has made me more conscious that there is trouble out there! It has made me very alert to the dangers. I have horrible thoughts about falling again!"

Older people also fall because of poor balance. The nerves that carry information to the brain about position progressively deteriorate, which affects their sense of balance. We can contribute to their security by installing railings on stairwells, providing bathtubs with handrails and nonskid mats, replacing slippery throw rugs, and keeping them from walking alone on icy surfaces.

Muscles

Our parents may notice that they do not have the same amount of muscular strength. Muscles do decrease in mass, so their strength is reduced. Loss of strength is also caused by poor coordination, which occurs as a result of changes in the central nervous system. An older person is not as quick to respond to stimuli and may interpret this change as a loss of "muscle power."

As a middle-aged adult we can encourage our older parents by giving them the needed time both to compute what is happening and then to act or react. From our supportive "take your time" stance (which can best be communicated by our own pace and attitude rather than words) they can feel that slower, deliberate responses are acceptable not only to us but to society.

We need to allow our aging parents to do *all* they are capable of handling, even though it may take longer or in some instances be painful for them.

Parents can be encouraged to slow this process of deterioration of muscle tone through exercise. Walking is the most usual and helpful, but stretching exercises are also important.

Rhonda's ninety-one-year-old father-in-law lives with her family. She shared with us the following example. "We have found out how very important exercise is in order for Pop to maintain his strength. His only real exercise is walking with his walker. In order to encourage this, I put a chart up on his door and marked it each time he walked a prescribed route through the house. It was a challenge to him and often he walked when he really didn't feel like it, just so we could put a mark on the chart. We aimed for three or four walks a day. This may sound like a rather childish thing, but it worked with Pop and eliminated having to nag him about walking."

Stomach and Bowels

Our parents are also noticing that their whole gastrointestinal system is sending signals that warn of changes in this body system. Heartburn, indigestion, and gas become more frequent sources of irritation and embarrassment. We might be able to help parents experiment with their diets so they can find those foods and beverages which consistently cause stomach upset.

Constipation may become a serious problem, particularly when unwarranted laxatives are taken each day. We can help parents understand that a certain amount of fluids and roughage in the diet will keep the body functioning normally without the use of over-the-counter laxatives and other remedies.

> Rhonda describes this concern as experienced by her ninety-one-year-old father-in-law. "Constipation has been a problem with Pop for years and he was always taking laxatives, suppositories, and enemas. He was under the impression that it was necessary to have a bowel movement every day."

Physicians point out that one bowel movement a day is not necessary for everyone's system.

Older persons may need to urinate frequently. This is caused in some instances among men by enlargement of the prostrate gland. Another contributing factor is that many aging persons are on diuretic medications for congestive heart problems.

If our parents begin to lose some control over bowel and bladder, or fear they might, this could lead to decreased social involvements out of anxiety over being embarrassed. Different types of reinforced underwear and special padded undergarments can ease their fears.

Marge was aware that an aging aunt was reluctant to go out anymore because of such fears. Concerned that this was reducing her freedom and her social relationships, Marge bought her aunt some sanitary napkins to wear when going out. Her aunt still expresses gratitude to Marge for this thoughtful solution.

Heart and Arteries

The cardiovascular system is composed of the heart and blood vessels. As a person ages, the heart begins to work at a slower pace. A weaker heartbeat reduces the volume of blood pumped through the body which in turn limits the oxygen supply. The end result is the feeling of fatigue experienced by older persons after completing a physical task, even a minor chore like taking a bath.

Let Mrs. Read speak again. "I got up Monday morning, cleaned the bathroom and then rested. Tuesday morning I decided I could do the kitchen floor. I got on my hands and knees as best I could and got finished. . . . Well, it tuckered me out and I haven't done anything since but rest." (This was spoken on Friday morning.)

The reduced blood flow is also caused by the narrowing and closing of blood vessels which have become more rigid and less elastic. This is known as arteriosclerosis.

As arteriosclerosis becomes more severe, aging persons have less and less endurance. They are much more susceptible to illnesses, and recovery time is lengthened considerably. High blood pressure, heart attack, and stroke are more likely to occur. Reduced blood supply to the brain begins to affect the older person's thinking capacities, and behavior patterns may change. Early detection of cardiovascular problems may allow medical intervention through diet changes, carefully monitored exercise, and medication.

The Senses

Human beings relate to the world primarily through the senses of seeing, hearing, tasting, touching, and smelling. All these senses are affected by the aging process and in turn contribute to the psychological and sociological adjustments to growing old.

Hearing

Hearing ability begins to decrease in our twenties, but we are not ordinarily aware of this gradual loss. Older persons may not be aware that this gradual loss is occurring or may be unwilling to admit that it is happening. This loss creates several problems. They begin missing parts of conversation, have trouble understanding what is said over the phone, and lack the ability to make distinctions between sounds (such as between the oven timer and the doorbell). These changes lead to embarrassing situations and contribute to the aging person's feeling of isolation.

We were visiting with Hugh, his two teenage sons, and his seventy-nine-year-old-mother. A close relationship existed and Hugh's mother was the subject of much teasing, thoroughly enjoying this time with her family. However, her hearing had diminished with age and she had to work hard at following the conversation. She misheard words or missed them altogether which meant she had to be corrected or informed in order to catch the humor. She tried to express her frustration humorously when she said: "It seems as if people don't talk as plain as they used to, everyone mumbles! They don't talk loud enough for me. Why don't you boys open your mouths when you talk so people can understand you!"

Many people can hear better with a properly fitting hearing aid, but it is not easy to persuade aging parents to try one. Their reluctance may seem like stubbornness to us, but to them a hearing aid may symbolize disability they are not ready to admit.

Whether or not a hearing aid is feasible, there are other ways we can relate to parents whose hearing is poor. We can touch them as we speak and look directly at them. Some older persons compensate for their hearing loss by lipreading. We can speak a little louder (not shouting) and more slowly when we converse. Be aware that noises, such as the television or the radio, are more distracting for aging persons and may be interfering with their participation in conversation. The telephone company can provide amplification devices that make hearing much easier and encourage socialization by phone. Just being cognizant of these few things could help us continue engaging in conversation with our parents, an activity that is basic to maintaining loving relationships.

Vision

Loss of vision may take several forms. First, a loss of lens accommodation may occur. The lens loses its ability to change shape, which means the individual cannot focus as well. Second, a loss of lens transparency may take place, often in the form of cataracts. These opaque spots on the lens interfere with vision by excluding light from the interior of the eye. Third, glaucoma may develop when the fluid in the eyeball does not drain properly. The result is increase in pressure which must be relieved or the retina of the eye will be damaged.

Most of these diseases of the eye cannot be prevented, but 85 percent of the aging population can be helped significantly with corrective lenses and/or surgery. Our parents may assume that losing vision is part of growing old and not recognize that such help is available. They need to visit an ophthalmologist who is medically educated and can diagnose and treat diseases of the eye. In spite of good medical care the eyes still begin to fail with age.

Thoughtful middle-aged children can help their aging parents continue to use their remaining eyesight by buying large print books. We can be certain that our parents live in a place that is well lighted and be more descriptive in our conversation. Reading materials, such as the newspaper or *Newsweek*, that have been put on records or tapes can be quite helpful. Keeping furniture and things they use in the same place encourages self-sufficiency. Make sure they have a radio to listen to if they cannot see television.

HEALTH CARE

We live in a culture that assumes physical health deteriorates with age. Even physicians are affected by cultural myths about aging. Few have had special training in geriatric medicine. They, like some middle-aged children, tend to dismiss the physical complaints and symptoms of the older patient as simply part of the aging process. "Well, Mr. Jones, you aren't getting any younger." "Now, Mrs. Smith, you have to expect these things at your age."

This reluctance of physicians to perceive older patients as worthy of serious diagnosis and treatment has been called "condescension medicine" by the American Medical Association. The AMA clearly states that age should not preclude good medical treatment. Many symptoms and complaints of older people reflect real diseases and physical problems rather than "just old age." These diseases and symptoms can be treated both medically and surgically, just as they would be for younger persons.

As a middle-aged adult, you may wish to learn more about

the physical problems and diseases of the aging. Educating yourself will enable you to interpret what is happening to your parents physically and to spot symptoms that need attention. A noted medical author, Lawrence Galton, for example, has written a book, *Don't Give Up on an Aging Parent.* He describes in nontechnical language the most significant physical illnesses of the aged and the possible medical interventions.

If you question the medical care now being received by your parents, you may be able to introduce them to a physician with special interest in gerontology. Your local medical society may be able to help. However, if your parents are under the care of a doctor with whom they have been related for a long time, from whom they receive sympathetic listening, and whom they deeply trust, you will not get far raising questions about his or her competency. Your parents will defend the doctor and question your wisdom. Perhaps you can work with this doctor in making a referral for specific concerns to a specialist in geriatric medicine.

Going with your parents to the doctor may be helpful. You might be able to ask questions or point out symptoms more completely than your parents. You might help them remember specific medical directions. If this is done with too much "parenting," however, your parents may balk, feeling that you are treating them as children "who don't have sense enough to get in out of the rain." Then, they may not only refuse your help but hide or distort their medical situation.

Instead of hiding or playing down their medical problems, some older people use them to gain sympathy. Occasionally they may even use their health problems to try to control the family. Before deciding that this is happening, make sure to get a thorough diagnosis.

We must walk that narrow path between being overprotective of our parents and being unconcerned or ignorant. Senior citizens clearly expressed to us their desire to be honest with their children about health-related concerns. They specifically appreciated the encouragement of their children in terms of preventive measures such as eating and exercising properly.

We must not overlook the psychological and sociological factors in good health. When we help our parents remain active, independent, involved with friends, feeling important and useful, and challenged by life, we contribute immeasurably to their good health.

3. Loss and Grief in the Later Years

Loss and grief are constant companions of aging individuals. They face changes in life characterized by words and phrases such as "fading," "impairment," "slowed-down," "gone," "used to," and "when I was your age." These constant losses wear and tear on both the emotional and physical health of our aging parents. It is normal for our parents to grieve over these losses.

PHYSICAL LOSSES

We have already described some of the physical changes taking place during the aging process. Did you notice how often the idea of "loss" was mentioned? Aging persons often lose weight, height, hair, teeth, strength, and mobility. They lose to some degree (or maybe totally) the ability to hear, see, and taste. Human beings are quite "tied up" with their bodies. When we lose part of anything in which we are invested, we lose part of our "self." Our parents miss and grieve those aspects of their physical self which are gone.

Societal values concerning the body and physical appearance contribute to this sense of loss. Americans, for example, worship youthfulness and sexual attractiveness. As they grow

30

older our parents lose their youthful looks and sexual attractiveness.

> Mrs. Read, eighty-one, was speaking to a group of ministers about what it means to get older when she said: "Sometimes I look in the mirror and can't believe it is me. How did I get to be this old wrinkled woman? I don't know how you young people can stand to look at us old people. Sometimes I'd give anything to be twenty-five again. Heads don't turn anymore."

For some older persons this loss of socially recognized physical attributes is a heavy and depressing event. Those who have emotionally tied their sense of self-worth to the altar of physical appearance and worshiped the gods and goddesses of youth, experience despair over their aging bodies. We have all seen aging persons use cosmetics, dyes, wigs, and inappropriate clothing in an attempt to maintain a youthful attractiveness that is no longer possible. Most of our parents will not take the loss of physical attractiveness this hard, but still they worry about their appearance.

> Mark's mother, now in her sixties, is the oldest of three girls. Her concern about physical appearance surfaces in her attempts to "keep up" with her sisters even though they are fifteen and twenty years younger. She often resorts to using extra makeup in inappropriate ways trying to look youthful. Yet she wears dirty, wrinkled clothes because she will not spend the money to clean them. She does not realize that her clothes detract from her appearance, although Mark tries tactfully to point this out.

We know that feeling good about one's physical self contributes to one's overall sense of well-being. We can contribute to our parents' sense of self-esteem if we help them use makeup appropriately, wear clothes that are clean and attractive, assist in combing their hair, and compliment them when they look nice.

Another type of physical loss is the loss due to disease or illness. A particular grief occurs when a parent loses a body function. A stroke may severely hinder his or her ability to speak or use one side of the body. Arthritis can cripple and impair use of the hands. Your parent may feel partially disabled when he or she can no longer do certain tasks like cutting the grass, going shopping, or climbing the stairs to the attic or basement. Older persons get tired of "something going wrong all the time."

Social Losses

Physical losses contribute to social losses. Isolation is a major problem for many older people. Losing their hearing separates them from conversation and other normal means of contact with the world around them. Imagine the sense of isolation you would feel if day in and day out you were unable to catch much of what was said on radio, on television, and in personal conversation!

When people realize that an aging person does not hear well, they will often fail to make the effort to communicate. Some people feel foolish talking loudly and slowly, or writing messages. Since both parties may be embarrassed and uncomfortable, neither may take much initiative. Our parents may tend to stay away from us and from others if they begin to realize they miss much of what is being said. Since we, as well as our children, may get frustrated having to repeat words and phrases, we might find it easier not to be around our parents. .Parents then feel "left out" and worthless.

Partial loss of sight may keep older persons from reading and watching television, which also contributes to their isolation. Impaired vision also affects travel and makes "getting out" more difficult. They must have help, which means asking for time and energy from another person, time and energy that seems difficult to give in this harried, busy society. The older person senses this and becomes reluctant to ask, fearful of imposing on others. Of course, this further increases the sense of distance and separation from loved ones and the world.

It becomes important for us to work consciously at overcoming these physical barriers and breaking down the isolation that can interrupt relationships and keep our parents from loving and being loved. We can do this best by "presence" and communication, "being there" in person, by phone, or in letters.

> One middle-aged couple, who live several states away from their aging parents, described their commitment to communication. "We consider it a tithe, or more accurately an offering, to make regular phone calls home. Long distance seems expensive, but the value per dollar spent is worth more than most things we spend money for. Mail has become increasingly important as they have gotten older. We send some of the children's art work and school papers to keep in touch."

Humans are identified not only with their bodies but also with their family and friends. When our aging parents are separated or isolated from these relationships by physical limitations and losses, part of their "self" dies and they experience grief.

Loss by Death

As people age, death claims more and more of their family and friends. Many of these relationships have been nurtured over the years and are very special. When the people through whom we extend ourselves die, we are wounded in our bodies, our minds, and our hearts. These wounds heal slowly. In the first two thirds of life we suffer these disruptive experiences once in a while. Our parents, however, are regularly suffering the loss of significant persons.

We were sitting on his back porch talking about friendship when my good friend and colleague, now seventy-three years old, said: "You must realize that at least once a week I pick up the paper, the alumni news, the church bulletin, a letter, or the telephone, to find that another friend has died. At least half of my friends and colleagues who are my age are dead."

We know how important it is to verbalize and share grief. Yet when parents are constantly talking about death, it is not always easy to listen. To us and to the grandchildren it may feel morbid. One teenager called his grandmother's conversation "the latest death count." A middle-aged son labeled his elderly mother's phone calls the "oral obituary column."

Loss of Work and Meaningful Activity

Individuals extend themselves into tasks as well as personal relationships. One aspect of the personal identity which our parents have carved out for themselves is the work and activity in which they are involved. When these activities are lost, a part of their identity is forfeited, resulting in a grief reaction.

At retirement, for example, many persons feel a tremendous sense of loss. Getting up and going to work every workday for forty years establishes a deeply ingrained pattern of existence. The work itself may give expression to particular skills and abilities in which an individual takes pride. A sense of worth, a clear perception of importance, and a feeling of belonging are often part of one's work situation. Giving up this support system, or having it taken away by forced retirement, can have a significant physical and emotional impact.

Even if your parent had prepared for retirement by developing other interests and hobbies, making plans for continued activity, and realistically facing the financial changes, he or she might underestimate the extent of the emptiness, loneliness, and loss of direction that can occur in the months after he or she stops going to work every day. Many persons, however, are unprepared. They have not built a social system to replace the "guys at the plant" or the "girls at the office." They miss these friends and acquaintances and the feeling of belonging to a group. Many are surprised at how difficult it is to find something to do with their time. They had not realized how much meaning in life work provided. When they are not going to work, they may lose a sense of purpose and the sense of worth that comes from having an aim or a goal in life.

Obviously it becomes important for retirees to replace what they have lost by leaving work. New ways of expending energy need to be discovered. Social contacts must be made that allow for new friendships to develop. Often we can provide parents with something to do that can be both helpful to us and also meet their need to engage in worthwhile activity.

Physical Limitations

As aging progresses, physical limitations may prevent your parent from participating in meaningful activity. Arthritis and poor eyesight may prevent your mother from doing the crafts she has always enjoyed. Heart disease may keep your father from working the garden as before. Wise children will allow, indeed help, parents continue as many of their activities as possible.

Fred's mother was seventy-eight years old when she broke her hip. After that her health was poor. Both her doctor and Fred, her only child, wanted her to give up baby-sitting and candymaking, which were her most exhausting activities. After she expressed how central these functions were to her life, the wise physician recognized that these activities, exhausting as they might be, provided much of the sense of purpose in her life. He allowed her to continue baby-sitting for selected families and making candy with several precautions about adequate rest.

Well-meaning middle-aged children often fret over a parent's activity, worrying about its effect on the parent's health. They constantly say, "She will kill herself yet, doing that." But maintaining activity is a way of feeling useful and having a reason for getting up in the morning. When middle-aged children do force a parent to stop significant activities they are often surprised that the parent's health declines and he or she becomes despondent. Having "something to do" contributes to both good health and longevity.

LOSS OF FINANCIAL SECURITY

For most of their lives our parents have been economically self-sufficient. They had enough money to meet most of their needs, and many had extra to spend on hobbies, recreation, vacations, and their children. In our society money carries power and status, but most important it contributes to self-esteem.

As our parents give up working, because of retirement or health limitations, they will find themselves operating on a lower income. For some the reduction is dramatic and, therefore, traumatic. One of the scare phrases of old age is "fixed income," because it puts aging persons at the mercy of that feared enemy, "inflation."

Finances may even be a primary reason why a widowed parent may want to remarry. If a widow feels economically deprived, worries about becoming a burden to her children, or fears getting a job, she may rush the dating process and marry quickly for financial security. If we can calm such fears and help a widowed mother evaluate all available resources and possibilities, we might prevent such premature second marriages.

After his father's death, Barry's mother was left with few financial resources. Because of her stated concerns about dating, Barry is certain that her primary motivation for remarriage was economic. He feels guilty now that he did not take more initiative to help her with finances.

Anxiety over financial insecurity is a problem, but we must stress also the emotional significance connected with the loss of spending power. When finances are tight, our parents lose the power and respect that money conveys. For more well-to-do parents it may mean having to stop buying new cars every year. We may not think that such a situation is important, but they may feel that their status has changed, and experience a strong sense of loss. For a less well,off parent it may mean not being able to give nice Christmas gifts to family and friends, or perhaps giving none at all. Being able to give gifts is an important way to express one's personhood in our society. To lose that ability is a significant loss.

This loss of economic power is usually more difficult for males. Our society has always equated "manliness" with the ability to make money and support one's family. When your father no longer earns money, or can no longer live in his accustomed style, he may lose some of his self-esteem as a man.

This loss of power and self-esteem are two of the reasons (along with the need for meaningful activity) you may have difficulty trying to persuade either parent or both parents to quit working. You may feel that they can live comfortably on what retirement income they have, but they may be more acutely aware of the potential loss of power and esteem.

Many middle-aged children experience frustration when their parents give gifts to grandchildren which are more expensive than they could afford. The middle-aged son or daughter may scold the parents for not "being more sensible." For our parents, however, the giving of gifts may represent one way of maintaining pride in self. Although their actions seem unrealistic to us, we need to understand and accept the feelings behind their behavior.

Loss of Independence

Independence is a prized possession for most people in our culture. Through childhood and adolescence we are taught to take care of ourselves. Self-reliance and autonomy are rewarded, and dependency, in most situations, is frowned upon. Persons who are independent and self-sufficient usually have higher self-regard than those who depend on others.

It is not surprising that most older people fight vehemently to keep their independence as long as possible. They want to live their own lives, in their own place of residence, in their own style. Most middle-aged children realize that this independence is best for everyone, both their parents and their own family.

Occasionally dependency comes quickly as the result of a debilitating illness or accident. More often it comes slowly. After one fall, for example, they may decide no longer to go outdoors in ice or snow. They become more dependent on good weather.

When ice and snow come, Mrs. Fulbright, seventy-four, will not drive or go out by herself. She goes to stay with her daughter, Dorothy, in order to have transportation and companionship during the winter months. Dorothy and her husband relate well to her mother, so this arrangement does not present too many problems. Mrs. Fulbright, however, often bemoans this new level of dependence.

As the years go by, your parents will probably experience increasing limitations on their autonomy. Loss of auditory and visual ability leads to increased dependency.

June (who had not married) and her mother (who was widowed) shared a mutually supportive life together for many years. June pursued a career and her mother took care of the home. As her mother moved into her mid- and late-seventies, however, she began to lose her eyesight, finally becoming blind. Slowly she lost capacity for autonomous functioning. She refused to go anywhere without June, and later did not want to go out at all. She became dependent on June for companionship and, because of her loneliness, she did not want June to go out in the evenings. It became dangerous for her to cook and impossible for her to clean, so June had to take responsibility for these domestic tasks as well as her job. Soon June's mother was totally dependent on her.

A stroke can limit mobility to a wheelchair and force dependence on others for getting around. In widely extended suburbs it is difficult to travel on foot. Therefore, when aging persons lose the ability to drive, they lose a measure of independence.

Since she drove her own car, Howard's mother, eighty-one, had been able to go to the grocery store, beauty shop, doctor's office, and visit friends by herself. She had not used the car much, but often spoke of her gratitude for the sense of autonomy and freedom from the apartment which it provided. She drove much less after fracturing her hip. As both her eyesight and hearing diminished she was even more leery about driving, yet she hated either to admit she shouldn't drive or to give up the car and the independence it represented. Finally, however, she called Howard and told him to come get the car for one of his teenage sons. She shared with us later the loss of freedom and autonomy she felt now that she had to depend on others for transportation.

After recognizing that their thought processes are slowing down, our parents may become doubtful of their ability to make appropriate decisions. They may become dependent on us for consultation and advice about domestic and financial affairs.

Many gerontologists believe that the most crucial ingredient in independence is housing. They find that most aging people desire to maintain their own residence as long as possible. The isolation of living alone, the fear of being in a vulnerable neighborhood, the possibility of needing medical help without being able to reach a phone, and other such concerns do not seem to pose as much of a threat as losing the autonomy which they have while in their own dwelling. Chapter 6 will explore the problems related to living arrangements for aging parents.

4. When One Parent Dies

The most crucial loss for one of our parents will be the death of his or her mate. Those who study stress rank the death of a spouse (or the last illness if long and painful) as the most severe stress faced by older adults.

A basic reason that the death of a spouse is so stressful is the increase in dependency experienced by most couples as they age. They spend more time together and are often each other's most significant companion and confidant. Older couples learn to lean on each other for help. One may hear better than the other and repeat social conversation and television dialogue. The one with impaired vision depends on the other for assistance when walking, for writing checks and reading letters. They count on each other's memory to take medicine and recall doctor's orders.

By now they have survived many traumas and shared many celebrations. In the most meaningful and happy of these marriages love has ripened into meaningful "one flesh" relationships characterized by sharing, openness, mutual care, and the feeling of being cherished. Even in more unfulfilled marriages spouses may have developed a grudging mutual regard and pride themselves on surviving together. In any case, aging spouses have usually developed a mutual dependency and feel a heavy loss when the mate dies.

41

The Impact of a Spouse's Death

Some older people try to prepare for death and separation. They talk about what each would do if he or she were the survivor. They live life with an awareness that it does not go on forever, particularly if there is an early warning that health is failing.

Barry's parents had a warning in the form of a serious heart attack which kept his father in an intensive care unit for quite a while. The whole family was informed about his critical condition. At first he was not expected to live. When Barry's father did recover, his parents responded realistically to his father's vulnerable heart. They talked over their life together, talked with the children, took trips together, and generally attempted to live the last years fully.

Other older people recognize at some level of consciousness the intensity of their dependency and do not allow themselves to prepare for the death of their spouse. They may refuse to talk about death with either spouse or children and generally behave as if life were unending. They usually deny early warning signs.

Although Sharon's father had had a heart attack two years earlier, her mother was completely shocked at his death. Sharon reported later, "I don't think she ever came to terms with the fact he might die. . . . She would not suffer that thought to enter her mind. Her attitude was that he either could not, or would not, die. . . . I don't think she ever dealt with any anticipatory feelings of grief. It was a total shock to her."

We will describe how middle-aged children can help their parents anticipate this crisis in Chapter 7.

Given the intensity of these relationships it is not surprising that the psychological wound is deep and recovery difficult. Bereavement is heightened by anxiety over the loss of such a major source of strength, companionship, and security.

Sharon described her mother and father's relationship like this: "He was the epitome of who she was. She lived through him. He was the glue that held her life together. She was very dependent on him."

The impact of intense grief on physical health is well documented. Studies of widows show that in the first year after the spouse's death they visit their doctors, enter hospitals, and have surgery at twice the rate of same age married women. The older the widow the more vulnerable she is to these physical repercussions. Many older persons, in fact, do not recover. We all have seen widows and widowers who gave up on life and "withered away" from no discernible physical causes after their spouse died.

CLAIMING YOUR OWN GRIEF

When one of your parents dies it not only affects the surviving spouse, as indicated above, but has a significant impact on *you*. The weight of your grief and the grief of a surviving parent will test your emotional stamina. It will not be easy to cope with your children, with your grieving mother or father and still find time and energy to express your own feelings. It is hoped that you will take the time to grieve this major loss, even if you are being leaned on as "the strong one" by the remaining parent.

Beth faced this problem upon returning from her mother's funeral. "I felt guilty several weeks after her death, because I couldn't seem to get my grief under control. Now looking back on it, I know several weeks is a short time to finish grieving when compared to the years spent together before death."

It is easy for you and the other children to be more concerned about, "How is Mom taking it?" than your own hurt. However, effectively to help your mother or father through her or his grief demands that you express and "work through" your own grief.

HELPING A PARENT WITH GRIEF

You can support your parents in several major ways. Perhaps the most important way is to allow the living parent to talk as much as he or she wants about the one who died. We know from extensive studies of bereavement that a major need of the bereaved is to verbalize and express both their thoughts and feelings about the deceased. Yet some children of a grieving parent will not allow the parent to do the extensive talking that is necessary.

"Mom, we've talked enough about Dad for a while."

"Don't keep thinking about her, Dad."

"Please, Mom, talking about him just makes you cry."

Often these statements are made because the middle-aged adults are afraid that intense mourning will be physically or mentally harmful to the parent. More often, though, the reasons for blocking talk are related to their own unwillingness to face the emotions engendered in their own grief. Appropriate mourning, even when intense, rarely creates mental or physical problems. In fact, it is the suppression of grief that leads to these problems later in life. Inviting conversation about the deceased spouse, rather than steering clear of the subject, is a much better option for everyone. This need to talk lasts not just for a few days or weeks but for months.

Some of our parents, of course, have never been able to express the emotional side of their personhood. They have grown up coping with emotions by controlling them. They may be embarrassed to share feelings with anyone, even their children. This trauma may allow them to break through that barrier. If not, we have no choice but to accept their preferred style.

One of the specific feelings a surviving parent may need to express is guilt. It is easy for the survivor to accept unwarranted responsibility for events surrounding the death. Reassurance about the realities can be helpful.

James and his wife described such a situation with his father, ninety-one, following the death of his wife after sixty-eight years of marriage. "The first few weeks after her death he had times of blaming himself. The night Mom died Pop had gone to the bathroom about midnight, and she evidently tried to get up. Then she fell back on the bed unconscious. She didn't come out of it. He felt that if he had been there, he might have helped but, of course, nothing could have been done. It was a case of heart failure. He also had regrets about insisting on staying up to watch TV until nine when she wanted to go to bed earlier, but would not go without him. We have tried to reassure him that he had been a good husband and taken good care of her."

The entire grief process will take many months and possibly years to complete itself. You must recognize that the death of one parent will significantly interrupt the life of the other for many months. This means, of course, that your life will also be affected.

Sharon's mother, as we have already described, had a deep and extended period of mourning. Sharon described how for hours at a time her mother "wept from the depths of her soul," literally "moaning and groaning" over her loss. Her mother had many problems to work through and spent much time talking with Sharon on the phone. How did this affect Sharon? Her description was: "It overwhelmed me. I was always, constantly aware of what she was going through. It was a great weight on my mind. It was like having a sick child. Even when you aren't sitting with the child, the weight of worrying about the child is with you."

The burden carried by the middle-aged children may not be equal. Often a parent willingly shares thoughts and feelings with one child, but not with the other. It is also common for daughters and daughters-in-law to carry more of this burden than the male. Social custom often identifies the woman as the comforter.

A second helpful reaction is to resist taking over and making all the decisions for your widowed mother or bereaved father. It is easy to feel that doing things for them is the loving thing to do. Of course some help is necessary and this assistance is a way of caring. To do everything, however, such as making arrangements, planning the funeral, deciding what to do with dad's clothes, writing notes, fosters a degree of dependency which is unnecessary and unhealthy for the parent. It may communicate to the survivor that he or she is now helpless and must be taken care of.

At this critical time in life, when severely wounded in heart, body, and soul, an older person will find it easy to move into more dependency than is necessary.

When Rob's father died his mother carried on admirably because Rob's sister was an invalid and totally dependent on the mother. However, when the sister died, Rob's mother went into deep mourning. One of her immediate thoughts was to sell her house and move in with Rob, Edith (his wife), and two young sons. They wisely suggested that she wait awhile. Although she did spend a significant amount of time with Rob's family, she came to realize that her own friends and a volunteer job were too important to her to give them up permanently. Rob and Edith were able to prolong his mother's independence and prevent some of the problems that develop when dependency comes too quickly.

Actually it is a good rule of thumb to try to postpone any major decisions during the intense period of grief. It is particularly important not to make decisions that create more losses. It is usually a mistake to change everything at once. Taking people out of their normal surroundings, away from friends and community, compounds the sense of loss and bereavement. Lifetime possessions become part of people's lives and are a comfort to have within sight and touch at such a time. Staying in the same residence, for at least a while, is usually helpful.

Another way of helping surviving parents is to help them (to the extent they wish and/or need your help) replace the many things which they lost when the mate died. Your father, for example, may have lost the one who cooked and cleaned for him. He may need someone to teach him both skills. Your mother may have lost the person who took care of the car and provided a sense of security.

Losing a mate often means losing social contacts. The deceased spouse may have been the more gregarious one, the one who made socializing easy. Grief and depression may keep one from taking any social initiative for a while. Many friends until this point in time have been "couple" friends. Now that your parent is a single, he or she will not be as involved with these couple friends as often. Starting a new social life is not easy, but you might be able to offer encouragement and suggestions.

June identified three ways in which her mother reestablished social relationships that helped her through the bereavement period which followed her father's death. First, her mother found a job as a seamstress in a department store. Every day she sewed and talked with two other ladies. They became very dear friends. As June said, "The job gave her more than the meager salary she earned." Secondly, several widows from her church reached out and took her under their wings. They also became good friends. Thirdly, a brother and sister-in-law began dropping by around five thirty each evening, about the time her husband normally had returned from work. They often ate together and became quite close.

You may even work behind the scenes to inform individuals and groups of your parent's need for community and invite them to take initiative toward your parent.

One of the most devastating losses sustained by a parent upon the death of a spouse is the loss of intimate companionship and regular sexual involvement with the opposite sex. Just the loss of physical touch is significant. Touching is one of the ways we communicate love and affection.

A middle-aged adult recently wrote these words to us. "One thing I think we need to be conscious of in dealing with older parents—especially those who are widowed—is to remember to be physically demonstrative at times. Touching can be important. Just a quick hug or a pat on the shoulder means a lot to them. I will never forget the remark one older widow made recently. She said that when the members of her church congregation held hands as they sang a particular hymn, it was the only time all week that anyone touched her. I think that is sad. It reminded me that everyone needs physical evidence of love, and that's not just a sexual need, but a human need. Sometimes we tend to forget this as people get older."

Loving another and being loved by another is a meaningful part of human existence. When this loving has happened in the context of a marriage over many decades, and death terminates that relationship, a significant void exists. After a period of grief many older people wish to regain such intimacy. After some months, or perhaps years, their need for, and interest in, companionship may lead them into dating relationships. We discuss this further in Chapter 8.

5. Changes in Our Parents' Mental Processes

Mental processes and emotional states are closely tied with our physical existence. Therefore, the physical changes described in Chapter 2 begin to affect the thinking and feeling of our aging parents. It is often more difficult for middle-aged children to be patient with changes in mental processes and personality than with physical changes. It is typical, in fact, for middle-aged children to write off these changes with, "Well, you know how it is, he's just getting senile." In reality most of these changes in mind and personality are an understandable part of the aging process. They make more sense when we take time to understand them.

The Impact of Aging on Mental Processes

The central nervous system, particularly the central processes of the brain, deteriorate with age. Our parents' reaction time is affected by the reduced speed at which the brain assimilates and processes information from the senses. Psychomotor functions like walking, writing, putting food on a fork, getting into a car, and opening a package take more time and require more attention than previously. The more complex the task the more difficult it becomes.

Intelligence usually refers to the amount of mental ability

a person possesses. Most researchers of the aging process doubt that there is a significant loss of *potential* mental ability. When older persons become isolated, lack stimulation, or get depressed, they may seem to lose mental ability.

It has been said, "You can't teach an old dog new tricks." That is usually because the old dog is neither in physical shape to do new tricks, nor motivated to perform. Older people can get in the same condition. Those uninterested in life or lacking stimulation will not learn (true at any age). Those who stay involved in life and are motivated can and do learn new things. Aging can slow learning, but does not stop it. Aging does not take away ability or innate capacities, and older persons resent being treated as fools.

Decline in memory seems to affect many older persons, particularly memory of the recent past. Most of us are aware that memory of the "long ago" seems to increase with age, while memory of yesterday becomes problematical. This may be related to the fact that the long ago holds more meaning for older people than does yesterday. We notice that those older people who still have interesting activities and meaningful involvements with other people do not have as much trouble with memory as do those who have chosen or been forced to give up activity and become isolated from others.

The process of thinking may also be slowed by the physical changes in the brain. This slowed process may appear to us as failure to understand. When a joke is told, for example, grandmother may not laugh. It seems as if she did not catch on, but when someone repeats a portion she catches on and enjoys the joke. The problem was not loss of intelligence, nor being "senile" or "out of touch." It just takes longer for the thinking process to complete itself.

Problem-solving is to use one's thinking process to apply mental ability and learning to the task of making decisions. This complex process becomes more problematic in aging persons. Conflict between middle-aged children and parents is often caused by the irritation the children feel when the parents are unable to make a decision. The parents may also feel frustrated at their inability to make a decision they know would have been made instantaneously twenty years earlier.

In summary, our parents will experience a slowing down of their mental capacities as they grow older. To what degree is determined by a number of variables. Certainly their own genetic makeup plays a significant role and this we cannot control. However, physical health and social environment also play important parts in this process. Everything we can do to help them maintain their health will keep the brain and central nervous system working at maximal levels. Nutrition, exercise, and medical checkups are important.

We can keep our parents stimulated mentally by providing reading material, discussing current events with them, and taking them to "happenings" of all kinds (movies, plays, parties, worship, reunions, and weddings). Involving them with people, new activities, and learning opportunities can stimulate their curiosity and intellect.

COPING STRATEGIES

We have already described the significant losses with which older people must contend. It is not easy for us to comprehend the impact that these losses have on our parents. To remain mentally and emotionally stable, they must develop ways to cope with the chronic frustration, the disappointment, the fear of deterioration and dying, the sense of rejection, the desperate need for identity, the loneliness, the helplessness, and the loss of control that may attend the aging process. Some ways in which they cope create further problems for them and make life difficult for us.

Denial

Denial is one defense mechanism that aging parents use to cope with the aging process. As they watch their friends grow older, they can accept aging for these friends but not for themselves. They continue to do all the things they have been doing even though it may be difficult or painful. Denial is all right in moderation, because it allows parents to keep functioning and feel useful. It only becomes hazardous when parents go completely beyond their limitations to the point of damaging their health.

Denial can be seen in other forms. Some older people will not tell their age. Others go to extremes in trying to look younger through the use of wigs, cosmetics, and youthful clothing. They may refuse to be involved with a peer group, because it would force them to admit to themselves that they were as old as their peers.

Suspiciousness

Some aging parents, much to our dismay, become mistrustful. They project their own uneasy feelings onto others and become fearful of them. As the elderly lose control of life and recognize their vulnerability, they can develop fears about being manipulated or tricked. Of course, older people do get taken advantage of, and some suspicion is a healthy way to keep from getting taken by assorted shysters, such as door-to-door salesmen and telephone hucksters.

It is easy for older people to assume that some of the negative feelings they have toward themselves are also held by others. They begin to react to others "as if" these other people did not like them. Often the middle-aged adult who has been the primary caregiver becomes the "target" of the parent's suspicions and anger.

Withdrawal and Isolation

Some parents try to maintain control of their lives by avoidance. Isolation becomes their protective armor. Everything else seems to be slipping away, so they maintain security by keeping to themselves in an environment where they feel comfortable and safe. Their fears and anxieties won't allow them to step beyond the "known."

> Evelyn described her eighty-seven-year-old mother-in-law. "I have tried to encourage Mother to make friends in her neighborhood. 'Invite someone over for tea. You need to take some initiative.' I've encouraged her to join groups with me or go to church. But she persistently resists my attempts to help her. I have finally resigned myself. Her choice is to stay at home."

Sometimes withdrawal is a way of handling embarrassment about effects of the aging process.

> June's mother became deaf in one ear and almost totally blind. She refused to go to other people's homes because it was hard to follow conversation. She was also fearful that she would bump into something valuable and break it. She did not like to be seen stumbling around, unsure where to step or sit.

Anger and Resistance

When elderly persons become obstinate and cantankerous, what is happening? They may be indirectly expressing the many irritations that build up at this point in life. After all, it is easy to see how an individual could stay chronically angry at all the frustrations, limitations, and losses that occur regularly.

Some aging parents use anger as a way of controlling others. It can be a strategy for maintaining some sense of power over their own lives. Hence, they will argue and become easily agitated or irritated over minor problems. As long as they remain angry they can feel like "somebody" whom other people must notice.

Parents may express anger through stubborn resistance to any suggestions or new ideas. To resist is a way of maintaining a sense of personal identity. Older people can be threatened by change, but often resist it as a means of expressing autonomy.

Reminiscence

Nostalgic storytelling is one of the stereotypical images of the elderly. Reminiscence is a natural process experienced by our parents as they grow old. We need to grant them the privilege and give them the time to share their memories of the past.

As they remember and reconstruct a past event, they are evaluating its meaning for their lives. For some this may be a painful experience as they recall old hurts, feelings of shame, injustices, unexpressed angers, and probably some guilt. Nevertheless, the past is a part of the present for them and being able to integrate the two in a meaningful way allows them to feel a sense of wholeness and personal integrity. This "life review" is part of their recognition that there is an end to life, that they are going to die.

The time of reminiscence is richer when our parents can verbalize their thoughts with us. Being an interested listener is a gift we can give. Often their own peers can enjoy reminiscing with them. Grandchildren like to hear old stories, especially when the grandparent can relate the tale to something in the child's life.

Rituals

When our parents do give up their independence, they can still maintain some sense of security by developing ritualistic forms of behavior. Regardless of their current environment, they can meticulously enact these same events each day. Daily routine enables older persons to feel some control over what is happening to them. By late in life, losses have become severe and preservation of what is left may become of paramount importance.

Middle-aged children may think that some of the rituals are unnecessary. Psychologically, however, those things which our parents insist on doing carry important meaning. Indeed, these routines often help older people maintain contact with reality and protect them from complete disorientation.

Our Response

All the behavior patterns we have been discussing will not be experienced by every aging parent. But your parent may choose one or more of these life-styles through which to struggle with the problems, threats, and losses created by the aging process. These coping mechanisms, though frustrating for us as care givers, can be considered normal if they are not carried to extremes. Let's look at some of the creative ways we can relate to these behavior patterns.

Keeping the lines of communication as open as possible is a crucial factor. The more we can help them understand, recognize, and talk about their fears and anxieties, the more we can genuinely empathize with them. We all know how much anxiety can be relieved by having a trustworthy, respected friend with whom to share. We can be that type of ·friend to our parents. We can also encourage them to develop such friendships and to seek out persons, such as a pastor, who can serve in that role.

We can respond helpfully to these coping strategies if we

recognize that emotional needs do not decrease with age, they increase! Our parents still need to love and be loved. They need to be needed, encouraged, and affirmed, just like the rest of us.

When our parents' actions or reactions do become so extreme that their overall ability to function is impaired, we must seek outside assistance for them and us.

MENTAL DISORDERS

Emotional problems can result from many causes. Often it is a combination of physical, social, and psychological factors. Emotional illness still carries some stigma, and middle-aged children may find it difficult to perceive that their parent could be having such a problem. This denial has caused many older people to go without the proper medical and psychiatric therapy which would help them return to happy, useful lives.

Wendell's sixty-six-year-old father was very ill with an undiagnosed gastrointestinal illness. For five months various specialists tried medicine and surgery to relieve the symptoms without results. Wendell recognized enough symptoms to suspect an emotional problem. So, Wendell broached the subject with his mother, "Mom, I think this problem is emotional." Her quick response was, "Oh, no, son, that can't be!" Her tone suggested that he should never think such a thing about his father. Then he said something about his perceptions to his brother and sister, but they both "reacted to it and dispensed with it as an impossibility." Wendell even raised with the physician the possibility that a psychiatric consult might be beneficial, but the doctor brushed off the idea as irrelevant to his dad's case.

Even physicians may fail to recognize symptoms of mental disorder in an aged person which they would immediately diagnose in a young adult. Instead they and the family are likely to categorize the irregular behavior or feelings as "senility."

Depression

Perhaps the most common form of mental illness among the aged is depression. Symptoms include changes in behavior, such as insomnia, lack of appetite, constant fatigue, psychosomatic ailments, apathy, strong sense of helplessness and hopelessness, exaggerated feelings of guilt and/or worthlessness, and suicidal thoughts.

Depression may mask unresolved conflict because it is often precipitated by anger which is not directed externally, but is turned inward on the self. We have already described many valid reasons why an older person would experience frustration and anger. Social training and misperceptions of the Christian faith may make it difficult for an individual openly to express negative emotions. The result is a feeling of self-blame, a sense of failure and of worthlessness, which leads into depression. We can offer opportunity for honest expression of our parents' negative emotions. They may be reminded that Jesus got appropriately angry (Mark 3:5) and that Ephesians tells us it is appropriate for Christians to deal with their anger (Eph. 4:25–27).

Guilt is often involved in depression. As your parents reminisce about their lives, they may uncover some guilts long buried, or revive regrets about decisions made long ago. They may feel some guilt about their present situation. Perhaps they do not consider themselves to be contributing anything to life. They may regret being a burden. If guilt is part of the problem, we may need to remind our parents of the forgiveness and mercy available through their faith in God.

Depression often involves changes in our body chemistry. Whether these changes are the cause of or the result of depression is uncertain. We do know that antidepressant drugs are among the most effective psychotropic medicines. Be sure to get medical/psychiatric help because untreated depression can result in suicide. If our aging parents talk about suicide, even in jest, we need to take them seriously. They are thinking about their own death and can plan an effective way to end their own life if they choose.

Hypochondriasis

Psychosomatic disorders are not uncommon among the elderly. Since many physical changes are taking place and an overall decline in physical ability is experienced, we should not be surprised when elderly people focus attention on their bodies. Enlightened awareness of body functions can prevent health problems from becoming unnecessarily acute or disabling. This concern can go to extremes and become a psychiatric symptom.

Hypochondriasis is the mental disorder characterized by constant preoccupation with health and body functions. If parents' waking hours are spent worrying excessively about bowel movements, diet, aches, pains, swellings, body temperature, coughs, sneezes, and other assorted symptoms, hypochondriasis may be their problem. Before deciding whether or not your parent is "imagining" a physical problem, be sure to have it checked medically.

Paranoid Behavior

If a parent needs to deny the onslaught of physical infirmities, hide from a growing sense of inadequacy and of worthlessness, or defend against fears of becoming mentally incapacitated, he or she may develop a thought disorder. The most common among older people is that characterized by paranoid delusions. The main symptom is an exaggerated suspiciousness that someone is trying to hurt them, steal their money, or control their mind.

When our aging parents consistently see, hear, or think things that have no basis in reality, it may be considered a psychotic reaction. We need to seek help from a mental health professional. They may have to be hospitalized for treatment if they become dangerous to themselves or others. Medication, combined with other therapies, can usually restore them to mental health.

Organic Brain Syndrome

Some thought disorders are caused by or associated with impairment of brain tissue and function. This condition is called organic brain syndrome. Symptoms of organic brain syndrome include impaired judgment, loss of memory, emotional instability, deterioration of the thinking process, incoherence, confusion, and disorientation. These signals may come and go. Some days your parent may seem quite alert, logical, and able to converse rationally. The following day, however, he or she may not remember your last visit.

Gerald's mother has been in a nursing home for several years. Gerald's wife described their visits: "Some days she is more confused. We try to tell her about something or someone in the family and she can't figure out who we are talking about. We try to straighten her out and in the next minute we have to go through it again. We repeat the same thing every time we go."

Impairment of the brain tissue may be caused by physical problems, such as hardening of the cerebral arteries, degeneration of nerve tissue, head injuries, reduced blood flow to the brain, minor strokes, infection, fever, intoxication, nutritional deficiency, and metabolic disturbances. Because organic brain syndrome has so many potential causes, it is imperative to have an accurate diagnosis. Many times this condition is reversible when the underlying medical problem is discovered and treated.

When a disturbance of the mental processes occurs, such as memory loss, much stress is experienced by the family. If the individual's spouse is still alive, he or she may find it difficult to understand.

> Rhonda described how difficult it was for her ninety-one-year-old father-in-law to understand and accept that his wife (Rhonda's mother-in-law) could forget certain things. "For example, he just could not believe that Mom had forgotten how to tell time. He kept trying to remind her how to do it. This was frustrating to both of them."

As a middle-aged child, you will find it difficult to accept that your parent no longer recognizes you.

> Jake's mother suffers from organic brain syndrome. She does not know that she is in a skilled nursing home. When Jake visits, she does not know him. The conversation is always irrational. It is extremely difficult for him to visit. "I can only stand it for thirty minutes. I always leave depressed! She might as well be dead."

It is difficult to watch a parent who is still alive physically, but with whom it is impossible to relate knowingly.

6. Where Shall They Live?

A brother, fifty-four, says to his sister, fifty-one, "Do you think Mother should live there by herself?" A husband comes home from a visit to his father's house and says to his wife, "I'm worried that Dad might fall and not be able to call for help." A physician calls the family together and describes the situation, "Your mother will not be able to care for herself again; you need to consider where she will go when she leaves the hospital." With these words, or similar concerns, middle-aged children reach a major crisis in the process of aging, "Where shall they live?" The question has to be asked more than once for many families. In fact, an underlying concern for many years prior to the death of a parent may be the question, "Are they living in the best place for them?" A number of changes may be made through the years.

After her second husband died, Clark's mother, now in her mid-sixties, did not like living alone in their house. She was particularly burdened by the big yard and worried about it constantly. After one year she moved into an apartment built especially for older people. She lived there by herself until she began to have heart problems. Clark and his family tried having someone live in with her. That solution created problems. It was difficult to hire people and when that person needed to be off, it was difficult to find substitutes. The mother was afraid to be by herself because of her medical history. The son who did live in town could not always be available. At seventy, after suffering a more serious episode of congestive heart failure, it became obvious that she could no longer live alone. Clark and his brothers moved her to a nursing home. Interestingly enough she moved into a nursing home that provided more skilled care than she needed. She could have stayed in a much more economical intermediate care facility in a nearby town, but chose to spend the extra money to keep her same doctor. After this doctor retired, she was willing to move into the intermediate care facility near her middle son ten miles away.

Many events can prompt a change in residence which is not forced. Your parents may have moved when their last child left home, considering the house too large to take care of or preferring an apartment. When your father and/or your mother retired, they may have chosen to move to another city or a retirement village in Florida. Change of residence, however, is often not by choice but forced by some crisis. For example, if retirement affects income and financial resources dwindle, parents may feel it necessary to move into a more economical dwelling or to a less expensive neighborhood. Lack of finances can force a middle-aged couple to take an aging parent into their own home.

One crisis that usually raises the "Where to live?" question is the death of one parent. The surviving spouse usually considers whether or not to stay in the residence in which the couple lived. Some individuals choose to remain, realizing it would be hard to replace their network of friends, church, and family. Others want a fresh start or would like to live where their children reside.

MAINTAINING THEIR OWN HOME

As we have seen, independence is very important in our society. It becomes all the more crucial during the aging process because of the contributions independence makes to self-esteem. We pointed out that many older people work hard to protect their autonomy even when they must sacrifice other values in order to preserve it.

Your parents are probably eager to maintain their own residence. They realize that with independence comes the freedom to control their own lives. To become dependent before it is imperative is to give up control over their own destiny.

Most middle-aged adults recognize the value of self-determination and are willing to help parents continue in their own homes as long as possible. The more dependent the aging parents, the more stress is usually created for both them and their children. It benefits both your parents and your family, then, if you can aid them in maintaining their place of residence.

Why is housing such a crucial aspect of continued independence? When your parents continue to maintain their own household it gives them something for which to be responsible. They must make decisions about when and what to eat, when to go to bed, and what to clean. Such decision-making, and the resultant activity, keeps our parents physically involved, forces them to flex their mental capacities, and contributes to their self-respect. Being in their own place provides privacy, another contributor to self-esteem. This autonomous functioning can be a major factor in maintaining both psychological and physical health.

During her eighty-second year, Marge's mother began to develop a health problem related to a chronic hernia, loss of blood, and low hemoglobin count. The resultant physical limitations made her worry about whether or not she could "keep up her yard" and stay healthy. She began to wonder, as did Marge and other family members, whether she should now leave her home. They considered two alternatives. One possibility was for the mother to buy her way into a retirement home where she would be taken care of for the rest of her life. The second possibility was to rent a small apartment in the same town. Finally they decided to help her stay in her own home as long as possible.

To make such a decision is not always easy. What are some questions to be raised when making such a decision? One consideration is the impact moving would have on your parents. We must remember the emotional investment they have in their home. They probably have many good memories associated with every room in the house. A rotting tree house where children used to play, a tree planted at the birth of a child, a flower planted as an anniversary gift, and the room where Papa used to sit are constant reminders of life's continuity and meaning. To leave these is to lose significant symbols.

Marge's family realized how much their mother loved the house she had lived in for thirty-five years. In fact, Marge's husband said: "The thing that sold me on her staying in her own home was when we got to her house this summer. The first thing she did was take us around and show us every plant. She had obviously given each one loving care and nurtured them along. She is proud of every flower, as well as her vegetable garden. She spends her day taking care of the yard. It is very meaningful to her, and for her to lose that would be a real loss, a heavy grief!"

Marge's husband is correct. "Breaking up housekeeping," as they may call it, can have a negative impact on your parents' emotional and mental health. Many older people have become disoriented, confused, angry, and depressed when they have to leave their home.

Another important ingredient in such decision-making is taking into consideration the desires and interests of the parents. They may know more about what is possible for them than you think. They know which arrangements make them feel most comfortable, secure, and happy.

When Marge's family gathered to consider alternatives, the mother was part of all the discussion. When apartments were considered they took her around to see several. In fact, it was this search which convinced their mother she wanted to stay in her own home.

It is important to our parents' self-esteem for them to participate in their future. It also keeps us from sinning against our parents by dehumanizing them or robbing them of their freedom.

Another major consideration is health and physical limitations. Is Mom able to care for herself? Is Dad in any immediate danger?

Marge's mother was in relatively good health. To help her feel secure the family arranged for her to make routine visits to a nearby clinic so her blood count could be checked regularly. They also hired someone to cut the grass and do the heavy yard work so their mother would not worry about how her yard looked.

You can see ways in which this family helped their mother stay in her own home. During the period when you are worried about your parents, but they seem to be doing all right, many private and public services are available to look in on them. Telephone reassurance programs make sure your parents are contacted each day, usually at a predetermined time.

If no one answers, the caller immediately telephones the responsible persons (family members, neighbor, social worker) so that a check can be made.

Marge's family arranged for a thoughtful and caring neighbor, one of their mother's longtime friends, to provide such a check. Each morning the neighbor looks to see that Marge's mother has raised a particular window shade on that side of the house. If the shade is not raised, she makes immediate inquiry or calls the youngest daughter who lives nearby.

Meals on Wheels programs provide one hot meal a day for aged persons. Such a service not only guarantees one balanced meal a day but also provides invaluable personal contact and a constant evaluation of needs. Other volunteer groups, churches, and agencies provide transportation service (such as to the doctor's office), shopping service, and run other errands for older persons.

Even when your parents become feeble or suffer from a chronic illness you can help them stay in their home. Some families hire homemakers who can assist parents with running the house. Your parents may need a visiting homemaker to come in only several hours a day to do some cleaning and cook a well-balanced evening meal. Your parents may become so frail that they need someone to live in who can bathe them, help them move about, give prescribed medicine, and see that they get proper medical treatment.

A visiting nurse association, or similar home nursing care agency, exists in most towns and cities. It can provide skilled nursing care and supervise those who are caring for your parents. This provides your parents with responsible health care in the home.

When Independent Living Must End

Many aged persons are able to live their remaining days in relative independence in their own home. Middle-aged children, however, are often faced with the fact that parents can no longer continue an independent residence. They must move to a place where they can receive more constant care and supervision.

A common crisis that precipitates such a decision is that of a sudden turn for the worse in the health of either or both parents. It is particularly difficult when one parent gets ill and the other wants to take on the care of the ill person but loses the strength and stamina to do so.

Gerald's parents were seventy-six and seventy-three when they began to have health problems. His parents did not want to leave their big country home forty miles from the city where Gerald lived. Gerald let them stay, but over the next three years his father's health failed rapidly. He would often fall and Gerald's mother would have to call for help. Finally, his parents realized that the mother could not continue to care for the father without suffering an emotional and physical breakdown. Gerald's mother needed to be free of the constant pressure and knew her husband would be better off if cared for somewhere else. They moved him into a nursing home in his hometown.

It can be even more worrisome when one parent is living alone, and the children worry that he or she is vulnerable to domestic accidents, break-ins, fire, poor nutrition, and sudden illness. Yet, the desires of our parents are very important.

After Gerald moved his father to the nursing home his mother wanted to continue living in their country home. Her eyesight became very bad. Gerald worried that she would fall and hurt herself or start a fire while cooking. At one point burglars came in while she was there and carried off some of her possessions. Still she wanted to stay. She told Gerald: "I know I will have to give up housekeeping, but I've got to think it through. Give me some time." Gerald and his sister reluctantly agreed. About two years later she said it was time for her to leave. With that word, she sold her house, all her furniture, and moved into a nursing home near Gerald.

This is an example of an older parent who was finally able to recognize when it was time to end an independent living arrangement. Other middle-aged children have to make the decision for their parents, sometimes against their will.

After her husband died, Martha's mother moved in with her younger sister, who had never married. The sister was a career woman who did not enjoy homemaking. The mother, then, took over the cooking and housekeeping. This was an excellent arrangement for both until Martha's mother developed a heart problem and her eyesight became very poor. Her memory became undependable. As Martha described it, "Mama began to misplace things. She couldn't do the usual daily tasks and my sister was even afraid she would leave the stove on. These things caused them to fuss at each other all the time. It just wasn't suitable for this to continue." The family got together, without the mother's presence, to decide where she would live. Since their mother had always dreaded nursing homes and asked them never to put her in one, they tried to think of other alternatives. However, one sister had small children, another had teenagers, and there seemed to be no place where she would be happy. They reluctantly agreed on a nursing home. Martha was the one who made all the arrangements and broke the news to her mother. She said, "It was very hurtful to have to put her in a home, but the children have to think of their families, too." The mother did not like the idea and it took her a while to adjust.

COMING TO LIVE WITH YOU

When it becomes undesirable or impossible for aging parents to live by themselves, one alternative is for them to live with one of the children. Many middle-aged children would like to bring their parents into their home, caring for them now as the parents cared for them in their youth.

Rhonda writes about their decision to bring James's aging parents into their home. "Our decision to bring Mom and Pop to live with us had really been decided several years before they actually came. James had begun to be concerned about them being in the apartment alone. Mom was pretty dependent on Pop in every way by then, and Pop had blacked out a couple times. I told James then that when the time came, I would be glad to have the folks come to live with us—but not until it was necessary—both for our sakes and for theirs. When Pop had a stroke that affected his left side, we brought them out here. It just never occurred to us to do otherwise."

Sometimes this is the only alternative that seems financially feasible. Other middle-aged children have never been close to parents or have had an antagonistic relationship. It is hard for them to imagine living with their parents under any circumstances.

Criteria that must be considered include: Is space available? Would the noise of children or the life-style of teenagers create insurmountable problems? Can the amount of care necessary be provided by the family? Is your spouse agreeable?

When older parents do move in, it is important to have

clear understandings in advance. What financial contributions will be made by the parents? What understandings apply to the use of the bathroom? How will the television be shared? What procedures will be followed when conflict develops between grandparents and grandchildren? Most important is the authority question. It is not easy for many parents to give up their parental authority.

Rhonda and James experienced the following: "Because of the kind of person Mom was, there was never any problem between us. But some difficulty has come because Pop is such a strong character. It's been hard for him not to be in charge. Pop had been the head of his house for sixty-eight years. It was hard to come under the authority of his own son when there was a difference of opinion about how things should be done."

If mutual respect and affection characterize the relationship, such arrangements can be meaningful to both parties. It can be difficult, when the relationship between your parents and either you or your spouse is distant or conflictual.

Moving to a Nursing Home

For many adult children the only alternative solution to the "Where to live?" question is a nursing home. Because of space, finances, geography, family commitments, or the necessity of skilled nursing care, having your parents come to live with you may not be an option.

Choosing a Nursing Home
In the selection of a nursing home it is important to check out all available possibilities. It takes considerable time and energy to investigate the quality and services of different facilities, but you will save yourself a lot of second-guessing

and possibly moving your parents later. Continue to allow your parents as much input into the decision as possible. If your parents are able, it would be wise to have them visit a home or two that you are considering.

How do you begin the selection process? First, understand how money determines your options. Know what amounts Medicare and Medicaid will pay for accredited facilities. Second, determine the type of care your parents need. If your parents need intensive, twenty-four-hour care, a skilled nursing facility is necessary. This means there are qualified nurses on duty twenty-four hours a day to carry out medical orders. If your parents do not require constant care, an intermediate care facility will be quite satisfactory and cost approximately half the amount. In an intermediate care home your parents will receive aid from unskilled persons under the supervision of at least one registered nurse.

Once you decide what type of home you are looking for, make your own checklist of concerns that you will investigate and evaluate as you visit various residences. It would be wise to check the overall licensing status of the residence *and* the administrator. Three broad areas to check for quality are: (1) medical, nursing, and therapeutic services; (2) food and housekeeping services; (3) the "climate" of the home—the social and psychological atmosphere.

How you are received by the staff when you visit is a good clue about the facility. If they show you only what they want you to see, it would be well to question this. As you tour a residence you can observe things that often determine the quality of care. Are the residents dressed and clean? Are they able to talk to each other and participate in some types of activity (not just lying in bed)? The way the staff relates to the residents is also important. Are they warm and sensitive and cheerful? Can you sense a rapport between the staff and the residents?

The actual layout of the building should be considered. Are there enough bathrooms? Are the rooms well lighted and ventilated? Does each resident have enough space to call his or her "own"? There should be sufficient storage space, as well as an adequate distance between beds. The general appearance of the rooms should be cheerful. It is usually a positive sign when you see personal touches that the residents have been free to give their own area.

If you would like additional information on nursing homes, do some further reading in Atchley or Silverstone and Hyman (see For Further Reading). Social workers know the strengths and weaknesses of various homes and can help you choose the right one. Your parents' physician may also have some ideas about which institution could best meet your parents' individual needs.

An Emotional Event

Institutionalizing parents is an emotionally laden event. Both parties are experiencing grief. The parents are mourning the loss of independence. Both the adult children and the parents grieve, because entering a nursing home is a poignant reminder of the final separation that comes with death. Both parents and children may fear losing the relationship. As is usual in a grief situation, many memories will parade through your mind, adding a wistfulness and sadness to the moment.

Mixed in with grief may be relief. The parents may feel relieved they are no longer having to care for themselves. They may be glad to ease the worries their children had when they were living alone. The children may experience the same relief.

Anger often attends such an event. The parents may be angry at the children for "putting them away." They may feel rejected and abandoned with the resulting bitterness. Their anger is hard to swallow. Siblings may be angry at each other about arrangements.

Wesley's mother had been living with his sister for a number of years. When she was in her mid-eighties, her health had failed, and it became difficult to care for her. Wesley thought she should be in a nursing home. But every time he mentioned such a solution his sister became angry with him, accusing him of wanting to put her away instead of taking responsibility for her. Finally, when his sister could no longer care for their mother because of her own physical problems, Wesley and his niece made the hard decision to put her in a nursing facility. Now the mother got angry, accusing him of not loving her and saying, "You are going to put me in the hospital so I will get sick and die!" Her words hurt, but Wesley had no option.

The adult child may feel angry with the parent because the parent did not take care of himself or herself to prevent such an event. The son may think to himself, "If you had listened to me in the first place and hadn't tried to climb those stairs, you wouldn't have fallen and made all of this necessary." Although difficult to admit, middle-aged children may be angry that their parents continue to live despite emotional and physical ill health.

Such anger usually leads to guilt. "How could I think such a thing as wonderful as my parents have always been to me!" The parents may feel guilty about continuing to be such a worry and a burden to the family. The family may feel guilty for putting their mother or father in a home. They may wonder about their unwillingness to "take care of their own" or question whether they should be more sacrificial and try to care for them in their own home.

If you turn these emotions inward, "sit on" them, and hide them from others, they will leak out in disruptive ways between you and your parents, or between you and your own family. You will be more at ease if you can share the appropriate feelings with your parents and your family. Other feelings can be discussed with a trusted friend or the pastor who may have handed you this book. Your pastor is trained to understand these thoughts and feelings. He or she can help you relate the whole event to your Christian values.

Relating to Parents in a Nursing Home

Life with your parents is not over once you have placed them in a home. You and your family still play a vital role in your parents' life. They continue to need you and want to spend time with you. Their adjustment to the new residence will take place more quickly when they know you are still caring for them.

If you live close enough to visit in person, do so as often as your schedule legitimately permits. Keep in mind that it is the "quality" of the visits that counts more than the number of visits. Rather than make a hurried visit once a day, when your mind is running in all different directions, decide on a special time when you can talk and relax with your parents. They will surely sense when you are sincerely listening and giving your full attention. If your home is too distant to visit often, your phone calls, cards, letters, photos, and newspaper clippings will demonstrate you are continuing to think about them.

If your parents are mentally and physically able, occasional visits to your home for a special holiday may be meaningful. Plan such an event in advance with both your parents and the nursing home.

Keeping close touch with the staff is one significant way you can help your parents. You know your parents' little quirks and idiosyncrasies and you can help to have some of these personal needs met by simply telling the staff members about them. You can tell staff members about special talents your parents have so they may encourage them to continue using the gifts available to them. For example, if your mom plays the piano well, they could call on her to play for special occasions. Your communication with the staff is usually welcomed. If you see some area of care going unmet for your parents, the staff also wants to be informed about these matters. The nursing staff that cares about their residents is usually eager to help you continue supporting your parents.

Nursing homes cannot meet all your parents' personal needs. If your dad has one favorite magazine not available at the home, be sure he receives it regularly. If your mom likes a certain kind of soap or bath powder, you can supply her with those specialties.

Along with the "things" you take them, remember your most special gift is simply your personal visit, as well as your family's visit. To make these visits pleasant and enjoyable, it would be helpful to prepare your family, especially small children, for what they will see, hear, and smell in the home. The sight of your whole family coming to share some time will help your parents continue to feel they are a part of your family life.

7. What About Death?

Some people are shocked by the unexpected death of their parents "before their time." Our culture develops the idea that a normal life should last at least past retirement age of sixty-five. When a parent dies prior to that age, it often catches the children without having seriously considered that their parents are mortals and would, like all others, die. You may have experienced that with one of your own parents.

However, if you have aging parents, you are more likely to have considered their death. Such thoughts usually provoke some anxiety and many persons are unable to think about it very long or talk about it with others. If an aged parent becomes seriously ill, then the fact of impending death becomes even more real.

ANXIETY ABOUT DEATH

Deep down inside we are quite threatened to think of our parents' coming death. Why? When we were children our parents were our first gods. Like other gods, they were perceived as immortal, and it is difficult to give up this subconscious perception. Yet our aging parents remind us daily of the fact that life moves toward a close.

Parents are significant persons in our lives. For most of us our parents played an unmatched role in our personal growth and development. We probably owe more to them and are more like them than any other persons. However difficult it may be, accepting that death lies ahead can significantly enrich these remaining years. Death is not an easy thing for most humans to think about.

Your parents may be very anxious in the face of death. How your parents think about death could be related to many factors. Research suggests that older people do not express as many death fears as younger people, even though their age, physical condition, and experience with death of friends would bring them into closer contact with death. One researcher suggests three reasons for this: (1) older people see fewer prospects for the future and have reduced their perception of their value; (2) they often feel, after living past a certain age, or surviving certain medical crises, that they are "living on borrowed time"; and (3) dealing with the death of friends, and perhaps a spouse, has enabled them to be more accepting of death's inevitability.

Evaluating how much your parent "has to live for" could give further clues. Older people in good health may look forward to many tomorrows, but upon the loss of health, the tomorrows do not look very inviting and death can look more friendly and appealing.

If your parent has specific purposes and ambitions, such as caring for an invalid spouse or a dependent child, a book to write, a significant job or profession, he or she will be more likely to see death as an intruder, and would be less likely to think about death. After all, there are more important things to do! In short, older people with good health, purpose, and independence are less likely to think and plan toward their death than those who are dependent, lack purpose, and have lost their health.

The religious faith of your parents may also have an effect

on their feelings about death. Research has indicated that people with a strong faith and confirmed atheists have less fear of death than do those who are in the middle.

James said the following about his ninety-one-year-old father's adjustment to the death of his spouse. "We have been amazed at how well Pop has adjusted to Mom's death. They had been married for over sixty-eight years. Of course, Pop has a strong faith in God, and he is sure that he will see Mom again fairly soon."

Even Christians experience anxiety in the face of death, the death of those they love as well as their own death. In his book, *Learn to Grow Old,* Paul Tournier recalls a conversation with his aging sister after she had suffered cardiac failure.

She had really believed, she said, that she was going to die. She had experienced terrible anxiety. And now she was questioning me because she felt ashamed of her anxiety, which she looked upon as a lack of faith. Should a Christian believer like her not have faced death with serenity? (Paul Tournier, *Learn to Grow Old,* p. 222)

Tournier, as both a Christian and a medical doctor with training in psychiatry, believes that anxiety concerning death is a universal experience. Every person experiences this anxiety whether consciously or not. His acceptance of this anxiety as a part of creaturehood shows in his answer to his sister.

Christian faith, I said to her, does not involve repressing one's anxiety in order to appear strong. On the contrary, it means recognizing one's weakness, accepting the inward truth about oneself, confessing one's anxiety . . . and still to believe. . . .
    I believe that there is more peace to be found in the

acceptance of human anxiety than in the hope for a life or an old age freed from anxiety. (Tournier, p. 222)

TALKING ABOUT DEATH

Yes, thinking about death is difficult, but talking about it may provoke even more anxiety. Many families respond to this anxiety by erecting a protective wall of silence around the subject. Dying and death become taboo subjects. If aging parents broach the subject, they may be quickly hushed:

"Oh, Mother, don't be morbid!"

"Don't be silly; you'll live till you're a hundred."

"You'll get better, Dad; we don't have to talk about that!"

It can be quite frustrating to older persons when they cannot talk with those they love about something as important to them as dying. Can you remember how it feels to have something important you want to discuss with your spouse, child, friend, or doctor, but the person keeps putting you off, or doesn't take it seriously? At some time or another, older persons think about dying. When their children will not talk with them about it, they feel isolated.

Why do people get anxious when the subject of dying comes up? Sometimes they are afraid it will "upset" the older individual. Many people in American culture are afraid of emotion and protect themselves from it by avoiding any conversation that might elicit emotional responses. Are you afraid your parents would get upset?

Do you envision that they would break down and sob? Or do you worry that they might think you were trying to hurry the dying process and be rid of them? Do you expect them to get depressed and morose? None of these responses is likely. You would probably find your parents would appreciate the opportunity to share with you. If they are too fearful to want to talk about death, they will let you know by changing the subject or pretending not to hear.

You are correct in perceiving that conversation about death can be an emotionally charged dialogue. Nevertheless, this emotion is not dangerous. Your parents will not have a heart attack or die suddenly because of emotion! In fact, sharing these feelings can reduce their anxiety. If you and your parents can be open about dying and death, this honesty can lead all of you to deeper levels of intimacy. Allowing expression of the related doubts, hopes, and anxieties will encourage them as they encounter death.

How can conversation about death occur? First, we can be aware of the opportunities our parents provide. They often give us an opening on the subject.

"I won't be needing that much longer."

"When I'm no longer here I would like you to have this silverware."

"It seems like every friend I had is gone."

We can answer with responses that invite more conversation.

"You seem to feel that life is getting short."

"Are there other things that you wish to decide while you are feeling good?"

"It must be getting very lonely for you these days."

Circumstances and events also provide opportunities for exchanging thoughts. The death of another family member, the acute illness of a parent's friend, a program on television, an article in a magazine or newspaper, or a sermon might give us the opportunity to describe our own feelings about death.

"I think I would like to die at home rather than at a hospital."

"I wonder why we are so afraid of death."

"I had a dream last night about being in an emergency room."

We can also use these opportunities to ask questions.

"What do you think Ellen worries about now that they have taken her back to the hospital?"

"Dad, do you ever daydream about your funeral?"

"What do you think heaven will be like, Mom?"

One friend of ours described a significant conversation between his family and his aged father which occurred when his six-year-old child innocently asked, "Granddaddy, are you going to die?" Many parents would have quickly hushed the child and with embarrassment changed the subject, but this family captured the opportunity.

OUR ANXIETY

We must face the fact that our anxiety (yes, we mean *us*, the middle-aged children!) is probably higher than that of our parents. As a whole their place in life probably forces them to deal more realistically with death. However, we are at a time in life when we are noticing that our own bodies are not what they used to be. We are facing clues that we are mortal, but we resist admitting this fact. We are definitely not ready to die and so we deny our finitude.

To talk with our parents about death is to make ourselves vulnerable to our own fears and anxieties. We might be afraid of the subject because we have not dealt with our own feelings about death. We may fear that *we* would get upset if the conversation turns in that direction. Perhaps we are really protecting ourselves by avoidance of the topic! Could we be instinctively covering our own fears when we say to ourselves, "I don't want to upset them"?

When our parents express concern about whether life has been worthwhile, describe what they would do if they had another chance, lament bygone opportunities, and admit regret over previous decisions, then we are pushed to consider the same existential questions. If we are pretending that we do not ask these questions and are avoiding honest evaluation of life, their conversation can seem intrusive and threatening. Cutting off such conversation or avoiding meaningful dialogue may be our defense.

Thinking about the death of a parent also creates anxiety because we realize that when parents die we become the older generation, the next group to die! This is an unsettling realization. Talking about death is also anxiety-provoking, because it reminds us of the emotional pain we expect to feel when our parents die. It may make us uneasy because of what has gone unsaid, both positive and negative, between us and our parents. Some adult children know that their relationship with a parent is not reconciled. Some anger may still be present from the growing up years. To talk about dying is to face these unpleasant wounds, a difficult task that many choose to avoid. Interestingly enough, the warm, tender, appreciative feelings are also difficult to verbalize. To think about our parents' death is to be reminded of these positive experiences and relationships which we do not want to lose.

Telling the Truth

This difficulty in talking with parents about death leads some middle-aged children to keep from ill parents the reali-

ties of their physical condition. Keeping such secrets can
interfere with intimacy. It is often difficult for old people to
maintain intimate relationships with those who cannot deal
with the subject of death. The fear of hurting aged parents
by talking about the medical realities is rarely realistic. More
often they are hurt by the conspiracy of silence.

Is it ethical to withhold information from individuals, even
an older one, that might prevent them from dealing openly
with a major event in life? The Christian must think twice
before deciding to deprive a person of information that might
allow him or her the opportunity for significant decision-
making.

It is true that some people do not want to know they are
dying and will not "hear" the message. This denial should be
respected, but not assumed. Aging parents deserve the opportunity to deal with their death even if they choose not to
accept those possibilities.

It is always sad when we (the authors) visit a family in a
hospital facing the final days or weeks of life for one member
without having the courage to face openly what is happening.
In the family's presence the patient pretends he or she does
not realize the situation is critical. But the patient talks to us
privately about dying and feeling distant from the family.
When we ask why there is no sharing of these concerns with
loved ones, the patient usually expresses a desire "not to hurt
the children."

Likewise, family members try to act as if nothing serious
is taking place. When they are with the patient, they talk
about the weather, sports, hospital meals, and everything else
but the important death issue. They also talk to us about their
anticipatory grief and the meaning their parent has for them.
Sadly, they do not hear one another's conversation. It would
be more meaningful to share these last days relating around
issues that are of ultimate importance and openly saying good-

by. Many things can be dealt with when death is not a taboo subject.

What Can Be Talked About?

When the reality of death is avoided, then life often feels incomplete. If our parents can bring closure to their existence, it will be meaningful to them as well as to us, their children. Your willingness to talk about death may enable your parents to make dying part of their living. Significant aspects of life can be discussed and shared.

Every day June visited with her eighty-five-year-old mother in the nursing home. On one occasion her mother calmly asked, "Can you tell me what it is like to die?" An interesting conversation followed. On another visit June's mother asked, "Where will I be buried?" She went on to describe her concern that to be buried by her husband would be too expensive. June was able to assure her that this could be accomplished without creating an economic problem.

Wills

Your parents may wish to talk about their plans for distribution of possessions. They may have imagined certain keepsakes, pictures, furnishings, or books, going to certain members of the family who would particularly appreciate them. They may be concerned that their death will cause jealousies and family squabbles. Explanation of their wishes while they are alive may reassure your parents that the family understands. Making these decisions can help your parents feel they have "tied things together."

Final Stages

Aging people may also need to talk about their fears of the dying process. They worry about pain, drawn-out deaths, being a burden, and indignities over which they have no control. Verbalizing these concerns with you means sharing them. All of us know that fears shared with significant persons are less frightening.

Such conversation may provide reassurance for your parents that you will protect them when they cannot protect themselves. They may need reassuring that you will not permit "heroic measures" or experimentation and will see to it that they are given pain medicine.

They also may wish to talk about what will happen to their body. Will they be cremated? Should they leave their body to a medical school? Or donate some organs for transplantation or research? Are cemetery plots already purchased? It is reassuring to make these decisions.

Another major concern of people in the process of dying is that they will die alone. Fear of abandonment and the sense of vulnerability to the process can be tempered by your willingness to be present with your parent as much as possible during the dying process. Maintain the intimacy even when conversation becomes difficult or impossible. Touch is important and can demonstrate your care even after verbal communication is no longer possible.

Funeral

Some elderly people like to plan their funeral. They have particular meanings which they wish to convey through the funeral service. Often they desire to give final testimony to their faith and experience. Favorite hymns, Scripture, or poems, are important for them to have incorporated into the service. Knowing what will be used in the service can also reduce the anxiety of the family during the funeral.

WHERE TO DIE?

When death comes unexpectedly and quickly, whether at home, on a trip, or in a nursing facility, there is obviously no choice about where it should happen. At other times a medical emergency necessitates a trip to the hospital where death may occur within a short time. One middle-aged male described such an incident.

My father had a massive heart attack when he was eighty-three and we had to rush him to the hospital. They did everything they could to save him. We were there with him, but there was no place for us. We were only allowed to see him for a few minutes at a time—never long enough to say much. We didn't know what to say anyhow. We were in the waiting room when somebody came out and told us he was dead. I wonder if he knew we weren't with him when he died—and that he was dying alone. (Barbara Silverstone and Helen K. Hyman, *You and Your Aging Parent,* p. 134)

However, some families have the choice about where an aged parent should die. Increased diagnostic skills allow physicians to determine more realistically the progression of certain diseases. In the latter stages of some illnesses further medical intervention is uncalled for, except for proper use of medication and skilled nursing care. Your mother or father, therefore, may not need hospitalization during the last phases of an illness. With pain medication and someone to care for catheters and other details, your parent may be able to come home for the last days or weeks.

For some, of course, the medical needs are often too acute for this to take place. Other families would find it impossible to take time off from job responsibilities to provide the companionship and nursing required, nor could they afford to pay someone to give this type of care. Others would experience such intense anxiety in the face of heavy feelings of responsibility and fears of the dying process that such an arrangement would be unwise.

If coming home to die is an option, you may raise questions about how you and your own children might react to such an experience. It is a misconception in our society that when people die it is always a horrible event. In actuality death in the situations we are describing is usually quiet and peaceful. Rarely is someone in extensive pain or frightened into bizarre behavior. We have seen so many real and simulated deaths through the mass media that the reality is distorted. We need to learn that death is not usually a horrible, painful, or brutal experience.

Most people today die in health care institutions, but many older people verbalize their preference for dying at home. Dying at home can create unusual stress and anxiety. Most family members who have gone through such an experience, however, report positive feelings afterward. Sharing the last days of life can be as rewarding as the sharing of any other significant happening. A middle-aged male experienced this possibility with another family.

I was always very fond of Tom's father and really shaken when I heard he had a brain tumor—an inoperable one. But I learned a lot from his family. When they learned that nothing more could be done for him in the hospital they —his wife and his children—decided to bring him home to die—to the house by the lake which he had inherited from his father. This was what he wanted, and they knew it. I thought it would be terribly hard to visit him, but it wasn't—even when he got much sicker. He lay there in his room, looking out over the lake which he had always loved, and he could hear his family in other parts of the house—

his wife, his children, his grandchildren—preparing meals, playing games, talking to each other. He could hear laughter and music. They didn't hover over him, but they didn't leave him alone much either—every once in a while someone would stop by his room to talk a little, to read, or just sit quietly with him. Even the littlest children came. I thought then, "What a wonderful way to die, with your whole life around you—past, present, and future."

(Silverstone and Hyman, p. 134)

By now you may have heard of the hospice concept. The word "hospice" is derived from a medieval word that describes a shelter for travelers on a difficult journey. It is now used to describe programs designed to control the physical suffering and emotional anxiety of those on the journey from life into death.

Hospice programs provide for care both in institutions specifically designed for this ministry and in the home. In either situation they involve both the patient and the family members in the treatment. Pain medication, for example, is either self-administered by the patient or given by family members. The hospice team is also interested in helping families deal with their thoughts and feelings about the dying process. Anticipatory grief is one of the dynamics which families go through while caring for a dying member. Hospice volunteers and professional staff help families through this process.

If your family can consider allowing an aging parent to die at home, find out from the American Cancer Society if a hospice program has been established in your area. If not, your doctor may still be willing to help you arrange things so that dying can take place at home.

WHEN TO DIE: LIVING WILLS AND SUICIDE

Old people may want to use a living will to help them gain some control over their dying. Many fear being allowed, indeed forced, to linger through painful, undignified disease and a long period of unconsciousness in the name of "the right to life," or in order to demonstrate medical technology, or because neither the family nor the medical team can bring themselves to end life for social, psychological, legal, or religious reasons.

Living wills specify the conditions under which people do not want to be kept alive by extraordinary methods, "heroic measures" as they are called. Middle-aged children can help parents express the fears, state their preferences, and get copies to family doctors.

On the other hand, some older people fear the family might allow them to die too soon if they become a financial burden. Others worry that they might lose the ability to communicate late in an illness and be allowed to die too soon. Others are concerned that the medical people would be overly eager to transplant organs they are leaving to others. Conversation about death can include the family's assurances about protection from such circumstances.

Older people can become so frustrated and depressed that they consider suicide as a way of controlling the dying process. Suicidal thoughts are often the result of physical conditions or depression. Proper medical and psychiatric attention will usually provide relief from the depression, and thoughts about suicide will subside.

Dr. Tournier calls death a "fearful and cruel monster." But when he wrote those words he was a healthy, active, seventy-three-year-old man. Both he and society would call his life useful and productive. If Dr. Tournier were confined to a bed in a nursing home, losing most of his senses, unable to care

A PERSONAL STATEMENT OF FAITH

I believe that every person is created by God as an individual of value and dignity. My basic worth and value as a person is inherent in the relationship of love that God has for me and not in my usefulness in society.

I believe that God has endowed me as His creature with the responsibility and privilege of sharing with God in the dominion over my earthly existence. I believe in the sanctity of human life which is to be celebrated in the spirit of creative living because it does have worth, meaning, and purpose. Therefore, I am responsible to use all ordinary means to preserve my life.

I further believe, however, that every human life is given dignity in dying, as well as in living. Therefore, I am free to refuse artificial and heroic measures to prolong my dying. I affirm my human right which allows me to die my own death within the limits of social, legal, and spiritual factors.

I believe I have the right to die with dignity - respected, cared for, loved and inspired by hope. I consider as unjust the continuation of artificial and mechanical life support systems through expensive medical and technological means when there is no reasonable expectation for my recovery of meaningful personal life.

In order to avoid the useless prolongation of my dying and the suffering of my loved ones, I am signing a document making known my will regarding my medical treatment in the case of my terminal illness.

INSTRUCTIONS FOR MY CARE IN THE EVENT OF TERMINAL ILLNESS

My faith affirms that life is a gift of God and that physical death is a part of life and is the completed stage of a person's development. My faith assures me that even in death there is hope and the sustaining grace and love of God. Because of my belief, I wish this statement to stand as the testament of my wishes.

I, _____ , request that I be fully informed as my death approaches. If possible, I want to participate in decisions regarding my medical treatment and the procedures which may be used to prolong my life. If there is no reasonable expectation of my recovery from physical or mental disability, I direct my physician and all medical personnel not to prolong my life by artificial or mechanical means. I direct that I receive pain and symptom control. However, this decision is not a request that direct intervention be taken to shorten my life.

This decision is made after careful consideration and reflection. I direct that all legal means be taken to support my choice. In the carrying out of my will as stated, I release all physicians and other health personnel, all institutions and their employees, and members of my family from legal culpability and responsibility.

Signed _____

Date _____

Witnessed by:

_____

_____

for himself, feeling embarrassed at the indignities of lost bowel control, and feeling himself a burden on his family, perhaps he might view death differently.

In the kind of situation described above, death is anticipated by many as a welcomed visitor. Dying offers freedom from the confinements, embarrassments, and frustrations of a life situation in which living is no longer of interest. Some institutionalized old people, in the last stages of life, invite death to come and may ask family and pastor to pray that death would come quickly. Others passively await the inevitable, but not without some anxiety. For some older people fear of being a burden on their families, anxiety over increasing disability, and an unwillingness to experience dehumanization and loss of dignity in later stages of an illness lead them to consider dying by their own decision.

Rev. Dr. Henry P. Van Dusen, seventy-seven years old, had been president of Union Theological Seminary, an active churchman, respected scholar and preacher. A stroke five years earlier had left him unable to speak. His eighty-year-old wife, Elizabeth, had undergone two hip operations and suffered from arthritis. They were becoming increasingly ill, needed constant medical attention, and knew they would soon be completely dependent for even the most elementary needs and functions. In the winter of 1975 they began planning their own death. They left a letter to point out they were making a responsible decision while "in sound mind." They described their situation: "We are both increasingly weak and unwell, and who would want to die in a nursing home?" Then they posed the question, "Does an individual have an obligation to go on living even when the beauty and meaning and power of life are gone?" They thought not and in March of that year ended their own lives.

Although many of Van Dusen's colleagues were sympathetic, his middle-aged sons regretted their parents' decision. It would be easy to imagine that if our parents decided to take their own lives, they would be rejecting us and our love for them. Certainly some aging people have taken their own lives because they felt neglected, alone, and unworthy. Others, like the Van Dusens, would not perceive taking their own lives as turning against life as a high value.

Getting competent medical attention for a depressed parent is our responsibility. But we can also be accepting of their decisions to take control of their last days. Openness about aging and dying may allow conversation in which these alternatives can be explored.

8. Family Relationships

The process of aging has a significant impact on family relationships. In this chapter we discuss the relationship of your parents to each other (their marriage), to their extended family, and to your children (as grandparents). Having older parents also affects your relationship to your siblings and to your own spouse and children. Finally we will talk about second marriages for widowed parents and the impact on middle-aged children.

OUR PARENTS' MARRIAGE

Our parents' marriage relationship can be for them either a major source of strength and comfort or a source of frustration and perplexity as they grow older. Whatever closeness they have developed over the years is now a double blessing that deepens with age. It is hoped that they have developed an interdependence, a "onefleshness," that nurtures both individual freedom and mutual trust. If your parents have this kind of relationship, it will aid them in dealing with some of the crises precipitated by the aging process. If they have been able to function as a mutually supportive team during past crises, they will be better equipped to handle the potential crises of these later years, particularly the stressful adjustments to retirement and life changes brought on by illness.

Retirement

The key adjustment may center around retirement. Until retirement each parent led a relatively separate life. Your father spent most of every day at work. Many of his personal and social relationships may have been related to his career. Your mother was either at her own job or busy as a homemaker. She participated in social activities in which her husband played no part. Even though your parents may have enjoyed spending time together and sharing important activities, such as involvement in the church, these affairs may have made up a comparatively small percentage of their lives. Of course, some couples survive because their lives rarely overlap, and they share very little except meals and a bed.

Retirement changes these carefully worked out life-styles. Suddenly your mother and father are thrown into constant companionship. They have not spent so much time together since they were courting or before children came. She has lost her private time and he does not know what to do with his free time. When they had such leisurely time together in the past it lasted only two weeks and was called "vacation." Now they have months of this kind of time which blurs the concept of vacation.

Your father's retirement can have a significant impact on your mother if she has been basically the homemaker instead of working outside the home. She has been accustomed to having her husband out of the house all day with freedom to plan her schedule as she wishes. She has been free to clean with no one in the way; now she has him "underfoot." Shopping could be done quickly and routinely; now he is along to pick up special items, question prices, suggest other meals, and in general drive your mother to distraction.

Many older women report that having their husbands retire is like having young children at home again. If he is lonely, he wants to talk with her. If he does not have anything to do, he wants her to help him think of something or do something with him. If he cannot cook, he needs her to fix his lunch. He may resent her church work, club meetings, and social involvements because he wants her around.

Trying to merge their lives again after all these years may create conflict. Either or both may feel that some of their personal identity is lost in the merger. How well your parents handle this stress will depend on their attitudes toward retirement, preparation and planning for this phase of life, the flexibility of their individual personalities, financial security, and the depth and meaning of their relationship. If your father anticipated retirement, developed hobbies, planned for using his time, feels financially secure, and retires *to* something not only *from* something, his adjustment probably will be smooth and stress on the marriage minimal. On the other hand, a rigid father who does nothing but work and watch television and thinks of retirement as an extended vacation, during which he doesn't have to do anything, will find retirement difficult for him and stressful to the marriage.

The attitude of your mother is also an important factor. If she has looked forward to your father's retirement and anticipated more companionship and shared living, then retirement will be of little threat. But, if she resents giving up her private life or gets little fulfillment out of her relationship to your father, the retirement years can be rough.

Kate wishes her parents could have made more of their relationship during retirement, but they drifted into patterns that could have been predicted from their earlier lives. Her father is quiet, shy, and passive. He has suffered one nervous breakdown and had problems with alcohol abuse. He does not enjoy much social life and hates to go places. When his business failed several years ago he retired without any preparation or planning. Now he sleeps late, watches television all afternoon and evening, and goes back to bed. For years he was an officer and treasurer of his church, but now he has dropped out of church completely. Kate's mother has been just the opposite. She is a highly intelligent, aggressive woman who owned her own business and enjoyed social life and travel. She recently sold her business and retired. She has now given herself to the pursuit of national competition in contract bridge. She spends time and money flying to tournaments with her social colleagues. Although she "fusses over" her husband when she is at home, Kate thinks this is to relieve the guilt she feels over leaving him while she travels. Of course, her mother feels hostile at his unwillingness to travel and be involved socially. Kate does not think her parents have a very intimate and satisfying relationship.

It is important for our parents to communicate with each other about their need for togetherness, as well as their need to pursue their individual interests. You can be instrumental in encouraging them to share their feelings and negotiate a meaningful use of time and energies. They may be able to agree on some mutually satisfying activities and still have the "space" to "do their own thing."

Illness and Disability

Another major stress on our parents' marriage takes place when the health of one spouse begins to fail. Exciting retirement plans can be wiped out overnight by accident or disease. A couple can be moving through old age with a full schedule of meaningful activity until ill health begins to overtake one or the other. Many older spouses, of course, expect this to happen. They are ready and willing to take care of the ill spouse. But caring for an ill person is no easy task. As long as it is an eight- or ten-hour task it can be bearable. However, no one—but no one!—can be a nurse twenty-four hours a day. When the care of one parent reaches such proportions you will have to intervene.

When illness becomes chronic or disabling, dreams must be forfeited by one or both partners. Travel and social involvements may come to an end. Getting out is difficult, and the well spouse may feel too guilty to go without the ill one. The disabled spouse, when uncomfortable with dependency, may take out his or her fear and frustration on the caring spouse. The nursing spouse may have a hard time dealing with his or her resentment over being in a confining and demanding situation. If the marital relationship was poor to begin with, this forced togetherness can become very conflictual.

Chronic illness can create a role reversal that is uncomfortable. Your mother, who has always identified herself as the care giver, may now find herself the recipient of the loving attention of your father. If he does it well, she may feel her unique position in the family is threatened. Patterns of dependency between your parents will be either strengthened or reversed, depending on who is sick.

As James's parents reached their late eighties his mother was becoming more and more dependent on his father because of her deteriorating mental processes. His strong love for her enabled him to take over her care. He felt affirmed in his role as care giver. When it became necessary for them to move in with James and his family, the mother's dependency switched to James's wife, Rhonda. She became "like an obedient child" and did everything Rhonda asked. This turn of events was difficult for James's father to understand and it "hurt his feelings."

Your parents may have enjoyed each other for a long time. They may represent those couples who in later years become very involved and devoted to each other. When one becomes ill, the other may wish to be the care giver even when the strain begins to affect that spouse physically.

Middle-aged children can underestimate the meaning of this dedicated care to both the giver and the receiver. They may institutionalize the ill parent out of concern for the health of the well one. Sometimes this is effective. At other times the well parent, now alone and worried about the care the mate is receiving, will deteriorate and become ill. It is probably best to help the care giver continue until he or she realizes the task cannot be done adequately.

Marital Conflict

Some of you have parents who have fought a constant battle throughout their married years. You may wonder why or how they have remained together under the stormy circumstances. Although they are unhappy together, they may be more discontented if separated. They may actually thrive on the discord they create with each other. In other words, psychologically they need to be at "war."

Another reason battling parents remain together centers around their moral/ethical values. Their belief system will not allow them to dissolve the marriage contract. They see no acceptable alternatives but to remain unhappy in the marriage. For parents with this outlook bereavement over the death of one spouse might be accompanied by a sense of relief and freedom. Guilt about feelings of relief may complicate grief in these situations.

Your Parents and Their Extended Family

It is a common phenomenon among older people to reestablish relationships with a variety of kinfolk, particularly siblings. You may be surprised when your parents begin spending time and effort in relating to brothers and sisters whom they had not seen in years. They may call, write, and visit with siblings with whom they had little contact earlier.

After returning from another weekend with his retired parents, Wendell made this observation: "I have discovered that my parents' relationship to their siblings is re-emerging. Mom and Dad are now visiting one of Daddy's sisters that they had not had anything to do with for twenty years! . . . Now they talk on the telephone and spend weekends together!" This renewed interest in siblings has led to a new ritual. It is important for Wendell's father to have Wendell relate to his siblings. Therefore, when Wendell visits his parents he goes with his father to visit his father's other three sisters in a neighboring county.

It is not unusual for this return to one's siblings to be heightened by the death of a spouse. It is startling to some middle-aged children when a surviving parent opts to live with a sibling, particularly a single sibling, rather than to stay alone or live with any of the children. Siblings will also take care of each other when physical or emotional problems arise.

Despite the fact that Dale's widowed mother worked, she also took care of her older brother, who was also widowed and chronically ill. She went to his house every other evening to fix a meal, clean, do the laundry, and check his medication. Although he had six grown children, Dale's mother did not feel they accepted enough responsibility for his care. She continued her routine until his death.

This closeness makes the death of a sibling a difficult emotional blow for our parents. If there were years of separation between these siblings, we may miss the significance of these renewed relationships and underestimate the intensity of the grief. This loss also reminds our parents of the immediacy of their own mortality. They may express concern over having the same genetic makeup and worry about developing the same physical problem.

Your Parents as Grandparents

Grandparenthood is one of society's prized roles. Indeed the relationship between our parents and our children is often one of the more rewarding aspects of growing old. At best, grandparents can relate creatively and lovingly to our children. They can provide affection and acceptance unhampered by the need to correct and discipline.

Grandparenting is often more enjoyable when our children are small and our parents are not yet old. About the time our parents begin to age, our children are probably in adolescence. This "mix" is not always very pleasant. The value systems, behavior, vocabulary, and boisterous life-style of adolescents are difficult enough for parents, but may be intolerable for grandparents. The needs of our older parents for stability, orderliness, predictability, and serenity are likely to clash with the gyrating, spontaneous, noisy behavior patterns of the average teenager. It may be difficult for your older parents to understand the freedoms and flexibility with which you may relate to your adolescents, particularly if they were more rigid and authoritarian with you when you were a teenager. Their disapproval, whether voiced aloud or communicated with looks and gestures, is not easy to handle.

Tom's mother, in her seventies, came to visit for three or four weeks at a time. He and his wife were raising their four children differently than his mother had raised him. She would lecture the children on what she thought was proper behavior and drive her point home with quotes from the Bible. She tried to make the teenagers feel guilty, insinuating that they were hurting their parents with certain behavior. Tom and his wife had to. be clear with his mother that they would do the parenting, she could do the grandparenting.

Whether or not our adolescents relate well to our parents will depend largely on how special the relationship was during their formative years. When grandparents become invested in our children during the early years, they can be more understanding of them as teenagers. Likewise our teenagers will be more respectful and sensitive to grandparents if they felt loved during childhood.

This mutual love and admiration will be particularly helpful when illness or long-term disability overtakes a grandparent. If your children have not had this sense of "specialness," they may resent taking time to make visits and feel forced to care for aging grandparents. Their hostility and resentment will be sensed by the grandparent and contribute to the grandparent's concern about being a burden.

Angry feelings expressed by your children will be disturbing to you. You may have some negative thoughts about your parents' indifference exhibited toward your children in the past. But if your parents did not give their hearts and minds (not just money) to your children, try not to let it "bug you." It was their choice.

Kate is a middle child and has always felt that her parents were partial to her older sister and younger brother. This preference seems to carry over to the grandchildren. Kate does not feel that her parents give attention or show affection to her children. When her parents visit, they bring one of Kate's nieces or nephews, the favored grandchildren. Therefore Kate's children never have special time with her parents. Kate is both sad and resentful about this fact, but tries to accept her parents' behavior.

It also would be unfair to make your children feel guilty for your parents' apathy or hostility.

If the relationship between your parents and your children is still in the formative years, or seems amenable to change, you might talk with your parents about how they would like to grandparent. A conversation starter might be the Westminster Christian Care Book, entitled *For Grandparents: Wonders and Worries,* by Myron C. Madden and Mary Ben Madden.

You and Your Siblings

During the time your parents are aging, especially during critical events like illness or relocation, your relationship with *your* siblings must be reconsidered. Do not be surprised if old patterns of family relating recur, many of which create stress and conflict.

Parents, for example, may have always looked to one child as the more mature, stable, and trustworthy. In time of crisis they may depend more heavily on that child.

Marge is the oldest of three girls and lives the most distant from her mother. Marge is seen by the mother as having better judgment than the others, even though the younger sister has always been the favored and pampered daughter. Recently the mother was trying to decide whether or not to leave her home and reside in an apartment. The other daughters and sons-in-law gathered to decide what to do, but the mother would not allow any decision to be made unless Marge could be there. In fact, she did not decide until Marge arrived, and discussed the situation with her.

In some families this could create conflict. Marge's family is able to joke about it. Some old patterns of dependency are outdated, but parents have a way of continuing earlier perceptions.

Leanne is the youngest of three children and has always been related to as the baby. Leanne is trained in cardiopulmonary resuscitation and lived only a short distance from her parents. When her mother went into cardiac arrest, however, her father habitually called the oldest two children first. By the time Leanne was called, she could do nothing to keep her mother from dying. Her father's old patterns of relating to the children may have cost the mother's life. It also left Leanne with a great deal of anger concerning the way her family discounted her adult skills.

Siblings also have a way of relating to one another as they did while growing up. They forget that each has become an adult.

Clark is the youngest of three brothers. During his mother's long series of illnesses, his two older brothers tended to make decisions and then tell Clark what they decided, rather than include him in the decision-making process. Clark, forty-seven years old at the time, said: "I was still the little brother. They were paternalistic. They still thought I was too young to have anything to offer!" This age-old pattern made Clark angry, because it discounted what he could have offered to the family in this crisis.

When parents and siblings relate with outdated expectations it can put a heavy burden on one member of the family.

Although Jake was the youngest of three children, he was the only male. His parents and his two sisters have loved and respected him since he was a child. His parents have looked to him for advice through the years. In the last year both his parents were very ill. Finally, his mother had to be institutionalized because of an organic brain disease. His dad's health declined, and he recently died. Through all of this Jake has been forced to be the responsible child and the decision maker for every problem. Though both sisters lived near the parents and knew their situation well (Jake lives two hundred fifty miles away), they insisted that he make the decisions for the whole family. The family's dependence on him became a heavy responsibility and created additional emotional and physical stress.

If you and your siblings are relating to one another as if you were still adolescents, perhaps a family conference is in order. Share with them your feelings about present realities, and how the situation calls for reevaluation of sibling relationships.

Meeting the Needs of Your Two Families

One of the difficulties for a middle-aged person is balancing the needs of children and spouse on the one hand and the needs of aging parents on the other. How to use the resource of time is most likely to be the major problem. More than a few families have developed conflict over the amount of time being spent on aging grandparents. Children can grow to resent the fact that they have to go to Grandma's house every weekend. "Do we have to go there again?" If you are spending more time with your older parents than your children, the children may feel that they are unimportant. Your frustration at being caught in the middle may leak out in anger at the children: "Don't you understand that Grandma is sick? Why are you being so selfish?" If you can stay aware of your frustrations, you can respond more directly and honestly.

Your spouse may have different feelings about your parents than you do. Your husband may resent the unequal demands placed on you and wonder why your brothers do not pick up more of the load. Spouses also feel abandoned and of secondary importance when an aging parent demands so much time. In addition, spouses may be feeling ambivalent and frustrated about the amount of money being spent on aging parents.

In any case it is important for you and your family to talk often and clearly about the conflict of interest. Your family might help you be more objective, and they need to understand your deep emotional ties. If the family can work out a mutually acceptable plan of action, it will reduce conflict significantly.

REMARRIAGE FOR WIDOWED PARENTS

Cultural myths have convinced many that as people grow older they lose their sexual interests and capacities. Jokes about old people imply they have forgotten what sexuality is all about. Not so! Older people, particularly those in good health, still fall in love, want intimate companionship, feel sexual stimulation, and can participate in fulfilling sexual activity, including intercourse. Older people often return to masturbation as the most frequent expression of their genital sexuality.

If you imagine that older people do not need the same physical intimacies that you do, you may be in for some surprises. When both parents are alive, of course, these assumptions may never be questioned. Children often go right on thinking of their parents as nonsexual persons. When one parent dies, however, these childlike perceptions may be jarred by the realities of the surviving parent's new romantic interests! It may be difficult for you, fairly content in middle age, to fathom your sixty-eight-year-old mother getting dressed up to go out with "another man." It may seem disloyal to hear your sixty-nine-year-old father describe the relative merits of two girl friends who are, after all, not even your mother!

After Sharon's mother finally recovered from her grief, she began dating. Later she began to date one specific person who became her boyfriend. She confided in Sharon the difficulty she and this boyfriend were having in deciding whether or not to spend the weekend at his lakeside home alone. They had been taking friends in order for everything "to look proper." Sharon shared her response with us. "I try not to think about it, and I want mother to be happy, but it is difficult to imagine her having sex with someone else!"

Your emotional response to dating may be relatively calm unless you become aware that your father or mother is actually sexually involved with a girl friend or boyfriend. Now that can be a shock! As children it was difficult for us to imagine that our parents actually participated in sexual activity. Growing up does not always change that subconscious perception. While our parents remain married we usually overlook the fact that they are sexual beings. When they become involved with someone other than our other parent, it can be quite disturbing. This situation sparks concern about infidelity. "Didn't she love Daddy?" Or "How could he do this to Mother's memory?"

Barry said of his mother and her new husband: "The first time we visited after they got married their physical intimacy bothered me. He was so 'touchy,' 'clingy,' and 'feely' it was hard for me to take. I had lots of funny feelings!"

Dating may spark other emotional responses. The parent-adolescent roles from yesteryear are reversed. Now the tension flows the other way. The same parent who may have constrained, warned, spied upon, and worried constantly that you would get "in trouble" or "get some girl pregnant" before marriage is now involved in exactly "that kind of thing." Dated anger can be surfaced by this unexpected turn of events. The anger can lead to jealousy and resentment. It may be a moral problem as well as an emotional adjustment to you.

Furthermore, our parents may choose to marry again. They may choose not to live the remaining years alone. Your parent could be choosing someone about whom you feel very comfortable. The care and love which they have for each other seems like a providential reward for your mother's ordeal with your dad's long illness. However, some of you may fear a mistake on the part of a parent who remarries. "Is he good enough for Mother?" Or, "Is she out to get Dad's money?" may be questions you are asking.

> Evelyn is sixty-one years old. Her mother is eighty-one and about to get remarried. When Evelyn wrote her own daughter about this forthcoming event she said, "They want Dad and me to 'stand up for them' in a simple ceremony. I can only say that I hope and pray it is a wise decision for them. We never know a person until we spend many twenty-four hours with them, and their real side is revealed. So as pleasant as Greg seems to be now, I do hope it will be a good union for them both. . . . I guess it's a case of loneliness winning out."

Money can become paramount at this juncture. Children often anticipate inheritance, without being consciously aware of such feelings. Some feel they deserve to share in their parents' estate. A remarriage threatens these hopes, because more of the estate will be used up in living and more heirs enter the picture. Some families use a prenuptial agreement to eliminate such concern and free the children from a sense of competition.

Most of these later marriages turn out to be meaningful to both parties. Like marriage at any age, problems occur and conflicts surface. The chances of your parent making a good adjustment will depend somewhat on the loving support of their grown children.

9. Reaching Out to Community Resources

As the number of aging individuals in this country continues to grow, our society is making a concerted effort to recognize and respond to the unique needs of this neglected segment of our population. Federal, state, and local governments have established programs to offer medical, financial, and social aid. Volunteer organizations and churches have become involved in a variety of services and ministries to the elderly. However, it is not always easy to find what is available.

Where can you begin? Several important publications put out by government agencies can aid in this search. One resource is the *Handbook of National Organizations: Plans, Programs, and Services in the Field of Aging* (U.S. Department of Health, Education, and Welfare, White House Conference on Aging Staff, Washington, D.C. 20201). This book will help you know which organizations can be of help and what to look for in the telephone directory.

Every state now has an agency charged with administering programs for the aged. Use *The Directory of State Agencies Designated to Administer Title III and VII of Older Americans Act* (Administration on Aging, Office of Human Development, Office of the Secretary, Department of Health, Education, and Welfare, Washington, D.C. 20201) to find the location, phone number, and director of your state agency.

Both of these reference books may be in your public library. The state office will provide you with pamphlets about current programs for aging and information concerning financial assistance. This agency can also direct you to the resources in your community.

COMMUNITY RESOURCES AND SERVICES

In some counties a network of services for older persons is set up and coordinated by the Area Agency on Aging (AAA). Check your telephone directory to find out whether this agency is in operation. The agency's goal is to help older people find the services they need. The range of possible services includes: meals programs, senior centers, homemaker services, income counseling, telephone reassurance programs, employment services, protective services, and visitor contact services.

To locate specific services offered in your parents' community where no AAA has been established use the telephone directory. Look for a heading such as Department of Human Resources, Department of Public Welfare, or Human Services Department under your local or state government listings. If you cannot locate the service you need, call your state Governor's Office or the state Department of Human Resources, and they will direct you to the appropriate place. These government offices usually have a toll-free number.

The Family Service Agency in your area offers counseling and psychotherapeutic services to older persons and their families. These services may be rendered in a variety of places, such as outpatient psychiatric clinics, hospitals, nursing homes, or family agencies. Sometimes the Family Service Agency may refer your parent to someone in private practice. Agencies accredited by Family Service Association of America must meet professional standards. You or your parent can check the status of an agency by looking in the *Family Service Association Directory* (44 E. 23d St., New York, N.Y. 10010).

Another helpful resource is the community's Homemaker-Home Health Aide Service. This is the agency you or your parent can call to locate someone who will help in the home setting. The workers are trained in household and personal care. They may be called upon to come once or twice a week to do specific tasks (for example, preparing evening meals, shopping, or some types of housework) or they may take full responsibility for running the home and caring for your parent. The National Council of Homemaker-Home Health Aide Services, Inc., publishes a *Directory of Homemaker-Home Health Aide Services* (67 Irving Place, New York, N.Y. 10003), which lists the places approved by this organization. About half the agencies are certified for Medicare, so it may be important financially to check on this certification.

Your parents' community may be helping senior citizens in a number of small, but financially helpful ways. The community may provide discount tickets for public transportation. Some supermarkets give food stamps at ten percent reduction of total costs. Movie theaters often have special prices. Some cultural events have special tickets for senior citizens. Drugstores in different areas offer discounts on drugs.

Many communities, plus volunteer organizations and churches, provide services and opportunities for senior citizens. Day-care centers provide a place where the elderly can congregate to play checkers, shuffleboard, and cards, work on crafts, or talk. Senior citizen clubs plan social events, travel opportunities, and involve members in projects that give them an opportunity to help others.

Many communities have developed special educational opportunities for older persons. Through senior centers, the recreation department, libraries, cooperative extension services, and the public education system various courses are being offered. "Financial Management in Retirement" and "How to Deal with Death" are examples of courses that may be offered. Write for *Learning Opportunities for Older Persons,* Institute of Lifetime Learning, 1909 K Street, N.W., Washington, D.C. 20049.

VOLUNTEER ORGANIZATIONS

Special service programs have been organized to give older persons an opportunity to volunteer their time and energy. In some instances they receive a small stipend for their work. The Foster Grandparent Program is an example of such a service. Older persons work in various institutions with children who need individual care. This job benefits both the children and the older persons. Other programs that may be in operation in your area are: Retired Senior Volunteer Program (RSVP), Service Corps of Retired Executives (SCORE), Senior Companion Program, and Green Thumb Program. To learn more about these programs and others, get the pamphlet *Older Americans Are Our National Resource* (Pamphlet No. 74-2081D) from the U.S. Government Printing Office, Washington, D.C. 20402.

Some older persons find volunteer work to be a rewarding task, particularly when it involves the skills they previously used or special interests they have nurtured through the years. To get more information about volunteer organizations that might be of interest, your parent may send for the *Directory of Voluntary Organizations,* U.S. Government Printing Office, Washington, D.C. 20402. *Volunteer Service for Older People,* published by the Office of Aging (U.S. Department of Health, Education, and Welfare, Washington, D.C. 20201), suggests places of volunteer service.

Religious Programs

Religious denominations offer many services and resources. The possibilities range from Golden Age Clubs to retirement homes. Some of the most common services are recreational centers where hobbies and crafts are done, fellowship meals, seminars for personal growth and education, and service projects they do for others.

Some churches are developing their own telephone ministry, transportation service for medical care, shopping service, and visitation program. Your parents may be fortunate to find a church near them that offers some of these aids. Almost every denomination has some agency that has responsibility for coordinating programs for older persons. The denominational headquarters or the minister in your community will know how you can find out what is available.

Older individuals may also enjoy publications written for them by various religious denominations. *Mature Living* (Southern Baptist) and *Mature Years* (Methodist) are just two of the possible choices in this area. These two magazines use larger print to aid their readers.

Reading Resources

Your parents now have more leisure hours in which to read. Along with the daily newspaper, they may like to read magazines that are written especially for older persons. The articles, whether fiction or nonfiction, usually are of interest to them. *Modern Maturity* is published by the American Association of Retired Persons (215 Long Beach Blvd., Long Beach, Calif. 90801). This organization also puts out the *AARP News Bulletin* and *Dynamic Years* (1909 K Street, N.W., Washington, D.C. 20049). The National Association of

Retired Federal Employees publishes *Retirement Life*. Other magazines that your parents might find informative are *Age* or *50 Plus*.

FINANCIAL RESOURCES

The financial picture your parents face as they age can be problematic for them and possibly for you. If your parents are willing, it would be helpful to discuss their financial situation. They need to plan for old age and you may be able to help them discover and secure all the resources that are available. Since the economy is in a constant state of change, it is important for your parents to periodically reevaluate their sources of income.

If your parents choose not to discuss their finances with you, it may still be beneficial to learn what resources are obtainable. A time of crisis might arise when you would be called upon to make decisions that may involve your parents' total financial condition. Knowledge about various resources would be invaluable.

Social Security

The amount of social security that can be received is based on the worker's average monthly earnings for a period of years prior to age sixty-five. The amount is determined by federal law and is subject to *change!* The amount received depends on several variables.

Your parent must apply for social security. He or she does not automatically receive it. Your parents may choose to start receiving their benefits at age sixty-two. This is possible under federal law, but the amount they receive will be smaller for their lifetime. They may choose to do some part-time work after retirement. This is acceptable under law, but they may not earn over a specified amount.

If you or your parents have questions, call your local Social Security Office or write the Social Security Administration (Baltimore, Md. 21202). It would be a good idea to check periodically at the local Social Security Office to be sure you are aware of any changes that have occurred.

Pensions

Pensions added to social security may permit your parents to get along without as much difficulty, though they still may not be able to live their accustomed life-style. It is important to read exactly what the plan includes. Often workers are unable to receive funds because of various loopholes in the pension contract. Read the fine print. Under the 1974 Employee Retirement Income Security Act, employers are required to pay at least a part of the pension they contracted to pay. A private attorney can help your parents collect. If a parent cannot afford such assistance, the Legal Aid Society in the community may be able to handle the case.

Supplemental Security Income (SSI)

This provides additional income through the Social Security system for people who have inadequate resources. If your parent is blind, disabled, or aged and is unable to secure adequate funds, the SSI will guarantee a minimum income. It is basically a form of public welfare for needy persons. Check the details for receiving this financial aid at your Social Security Office.

Indirect Noncash Supplements

Your parents can find out what supplements are obtainable in their community by calling the Human Services Department. In some areas tax exemptions are granted at federal and state levels. Your parents can check to see if government food stamps are available or if there is a commodity distribution program. Some communities have special projects for providing meals (congregate or home-delivered).

Medicare

Medicare is a federal health insurance program that your parents are entitled to receive once they have applied for it. They do not automatically receive it, nor is it free. Your parents must pay monthly premiums in order to maintain a Medicare policy.

Much confusion exists concerning what Medicare will cover, so it would be wise to read the details. For example, it would be important for them to know that every Medicare recipient is responsible for a deductible amount, which means all medical expenses are *not* covered. Certain medical services, such as homemaker services, dental care, drugs, eyeglasses, and foot care, are not included under Medicare. To have a clear understanding of this insurance program, ask for *Your Medicare Handbook* at any Social Security Office.

Private Insurance

Purchase private medical insurance if at all possible. Private health protection can help defray costs that are not covered by Medicare. As you read about Medicare you can see that the very items not covered are services often needed by older persons.

Medicaid

This is an assistance program for needy persons of any age. Federal and state funds are used to operate the program. Each state administers the funds, which means the kind of assistance available varies with the location. Services include inpatient hospital care, outpatient hospital services, lab and X-ray services, skilled nursing facilities, and home-health care services. To see what optional services are rendered in your community, call the Department of Welfare or the Department of Social Services. To receive financial help under this program you must apply for it!

Other Resources

As living costs continue to increase and your parents' fixed income looks smaller, we thought it would be useful to reiterate some ways your parents may be able to help themselves. Some older persons choose to continue working part time outside the home. This may be an option for your parents if health permits. Sheltered workshops also offer an opportunity to earn a small amount of money.

Health and transportation may prohibit leaving home. External circumstances may limit your parents, but there are still ways they can work and save within the confines of their home. Your mother may be skilled at a craft that she can make and sell. The book *How to Earn More Money from Your Crafts,* by Merle E. Dowd (Doubleday & Co., 1976), might be of interest to her. Your father could tend a small vegetable garden, which could provide a supply of nutritious vegetables. Your parents could do more cooking from scratch instead of paying high prices for prepackaged foods. They may want to look into the possibility of forming a food co-op plan with several other older couples. They can save a considerable amount of money by shopping in quantity.

We have described a variety of resources that may be available in your parents' community. Obviously our list is limited. Ministers, counselors, social workers, or nurses who care for elderly persons may be able to guide you to the services you are seeking. Another rich source of knowledgeable information is the older people living right around you. They know from firsthand experience what is available and which programs are most beneficial.

For Further Reading

The following books could be helpful in pursuing your interest in understanding and relating to your aging parents. They are nontechnical, but well researched, and very readable.

Abernethy, Jean B. *Old Is Not a Four-Letter Word!* Abingdon Press, 1975.

Atchley, Robert C. *The Social Forces in Later Life,* 2d ed. Wadsworth Publishing Co., 1977.

Birren, James E. *The Psychology of Aging.* Prentice-Hall, 1964.

Buckley, Mary. *The Aged Are People, Too.* Kennikat Press, 1972.

Butler, Robert N. *Why Survive? Being Old in America.* Harper & Row, 1975.

Butler, Robert N., and Lewis, Myrna. *Aging and Mental Health.* C. V. Mosby Co., 1973.

Deeken, Alfons. *Growing Old, and How to Cope with It.* Paulist/Newman Press, 1972.

Fritz, Dorothy B. *Growing Old Is a Family Affair.* John Knox Press, 1972.

Galton, Lawrence N. *Don't Give Up on an Aging Parent.* Crown Publishers, 1975.

Halpern, Howard M. *Cutting Loose: An Adult Guide to Coming to Terms with Your Parents.* Simon & Schuster, 1976.

Kalish, Richard A. *Late Adulthood: Perspectives on Human Development.* Brooks/Cole Publishing Co., 1975.

Knopf, Olga. *Successful Aging.* G. K. Hall & Co., 1977.

Loether, Herman J. *Problems of Aging: Sociological and Social Psychological Perspectives.* Dickenson Publishers, 1967.

Moss, Frank E., and Halamandaris, Val J. *Too Old, Too Sick, Too Bad: Nursing Homes in America.* Germantown, Md.: Aspen Systems Corp., 1977.

Poe, William D. *The Old Person in Your Home.* Charles Scribner's Sons, 1969.

Silverstone, Barbara, and Hyman, Helen K. *You and Your Aging Parent.* Pantheon Books, 1976.

Steele, Harold C., and Crow, Charles B. *How to Deal with Aging and the Elderly.* Strode Publishers, 1970.

Tournier, Paul. *Learn to Grow Old.* Harper & Row, 1972.